Workshop on Relational Models of Semantics 2011

AA004664

(RELMS 2011)

Held at ACL HLT 2011

Portland, Oregon, USA
23 June 2011

ISBN: 978-1-61839-231-2

Printed from e-media with permission by:

Curran Associates, Inc.
57 Morehouse Lane
Red Hook, NY 12571

CURRAN ASSOCIATES INC. proceedings.com

Some format issues inherent in the e-media version may also appear in this print version.

Printed by Curran Associates, Inc. (2011)

For permission requests, please contact the Association for Computational Linguistics at the address below.

Association for Computational Linguistics
209 N. Eighth Street
Stroudsburg, Pennsylvania 18360

Phone: 1-570-476-8006
Fax: 1-570-476-0860

acl@aclweb.org

Additional copies of this publication are available from:

Curran Associates, Inc.
57 Morehouse Lane
Red Hook, NY 12571 USA
Phone: 845-758-0400
Fax: 845-758-2634
Email: curran@proceedings.com
Web: www.proceedings.com

Preface

The ACL 2011 Workshop on *Relational Models of Semantics* (RELMS 2011) took place on June 23, 2011 in Portland, Oregon, USA, immediately following the 49th Annual Meeting of the Association for Computational Linguistics: Human Language Technologies (ACL 2011).

We had envisioned the workshop as a meeting place for those concerned with a view of semantics deeper than what a word or a collocation carry in text. A non-trivial text describes relations among the entities and events to which it refers. While models of meaning which focus on the lexical stratum are undoubtedly important, it is relations that bind individual pieces together.

The modelling of semantic relations has taken a variety of forms in natural language processing. Ontology learning and information extraction focus on learning "encyclopedic" relations between entities in the domain of the discourse. Structured prediction tasks such as semantic role labelling or biomedical event extraction require reasoning about the relational content of a text: which entities and events mentioned are interrelated. The interpretation of compound nouns – in the presence of little contextual knowledge – benefits from recognizing probable and plausible relations between two entities. And so on.

Reality seldom lives up to expectations, so we have been fortunate to receive a number of good submissions. The participants found out how rich language resources can advance the cause of deep semantic analysis (the invited talk by Martha Palmer and the paper by Coyne et al.) and how such resources can be built up (Ayşe et al. and Bonial et al.). They further heard about discovering elements implicit in texts (Tonelli and Delmonte, Gerber and Chai). There were also papers on classifying relations (Choi, Palmer and Jamison), on information extraction (Surdeanu et al.) and even on the connection between relations and sentiment (Kolya et al.). We thank the Authors for letting us put together such an interestingly varied program.

The success of the workshop was only possible with the support of all of the authors who submitted their papers for review and then presented them, the program committee members who constructively assessed the submissions, the invited speaker (Martha Palmer) and the panelists (Timothy Baldwin, Eduard Hovy, Saif Mohammad, and Sebastian Riedel) who shared their views on interesting topics, and the registered participants. We thank them all for their support for this workshop.

The RELMS 2011 co-organizers:
Su Nam Kim, Zornitsa Kozareva, Preslav Nakov, Diarmuid Ó Séaghdha, Sebastian Padó, and Stan Szpakowicz

Organization

The ACL 2011 Workshop on Relational Models of Semantics (RELMS 2011) was endorsed by SIGLEX: The Special Interest Group on the Lexicon of the Association for Computational Linguistics.

Organizers:

Su Nam Kim, The Univeristy of Melbourne, Australia
Zornitsa Kozareva, University of Southern California, USA
Preslav Nakov, National University of Singapore, Singapore
Diarmuid Ó Séaghdha, University of Cambridge, UK
Sebastian Padó, Universität Heidelberg, Germany
Stan Szpakowicz, University of Ottawa, Canada

Program Committee:

Eneko Agirre, University of the Basque Country, Spain
Timothy Baldwin, The University of Melbourne, Australia
Ken Barker, University of Texas at Austin, USA
Paul Buitelaar, National University of Ireland, Galway, Ireland
Nathanael Chambers, Stanford University, USA
Yee Seng Chan, University of Illinois at Urbana-Champaign, USA
Mark Craven, University of Wisconsin-Madison, USA
Matthew Gerber, Michigan State University, USA
Roxana Girju, University of Illinois at Urbana-Champaign, USA
Sanda Harabagiu, University of Texas at Dallas, USA
Iris Hendrickx, University of Lisboa, Portugal
Raphael Hoffmann, University of Washington, USA
Sophia Katrenko, University of Amsterdam, The Netherlands
Roman Klinger, Fraunhofer Institute for Algorithms and Scientific Computing, Germany
Milen Kouylekov, Celi SRL Torino, Italy
Kenneth Litkowski, CL Research, USA
Dan Moldovan, University of Texas at Dallas, USA
Vivi Nastase, HITS gGmbH, Germany
Roberto Navigli, Sapienza University of Rome, Italy
Patrick Pantel, Microsoft Research, USA
Marco Pennacchiotti, Yahoo! Inc., USA
Simone Paolo Ponzetto, University of Heidelberg, Germany
Sampo Pyysalo, University of Tokyo, Japan
Sebastian Riedel, University of Massachusetts-Amherst, USA
Alan Ritter, University of Washington, USA
Lorenza Romano, Cross Library Services srl, Italy
Dan Roth, University of Illinois at Urbana Champaign, USA
Barbara Rosario, Intel Labs, USA

Caroline Sporleder, Saarland University, Germany
Carlo Strapparava, FBK-irst, Italy
György Szarvas, Technical University of Darmstadt, Germany
Peter Turney, National Research Council of Canada, Canada
Benjamin Van Durme, Johns Hopkins University, USA
Tony Veale, University College Dublin, Ireland
Andreas Vlachos, University of Wisconsin-Madison, USA
Rui Wang, DFKI GmbH, Germany
Limin Yao, University of Massachusetts Amherst, USA
Deniz Yuret, Koç University, Turkey

Additional Reviewers:

Brian Davis, National University of Ireland, Galway, Ireland

Invited Speaker:

Martha Palmer, University of Colorado, USA

Panelists:

Timothy Baldwin, The University of Melbourne, Australia
Eduard Hovy, University of Southern California, USA
Saif Mohammad, National Research Council, Canada
Sebastian Riedel, University of Massachusetts, USA

Table of Contents

RELMS'2011 Workshop Program

Thursday: June 23, 2011

09:00-09:05 **Welcome**

09:05-10:30 **Session 1**

(09:05-10:05)
Invited Talk
Going Beyond Shallow Semantics
Martha Palmer, University of Colorado

(10:05-10:30)
Customizing an Information Extraction System to a New Domain
Mihai Surdeanu, David McClosky, Mason Smith, Andrey Gusev and Christopher Manning

10:30-11:00 Morning break

11:00-12:15 **Session 2**

(11:00-11:25)
Extraction of Semantic Word Relations in Turkish from Dictionary Definitions
Şerbetçi Ayşe, Orhan Zeynep and Pehlivan İlknur

(11:25-11:50)
Identifying Event – Sentiment Association using Lexical Equivalence and Co-reference Approaches
Anup Kolya, Dipankar Das, Asif Ekbal and Sivaji Bandyopadhyay

(11:50-12:15)
VigNet: Grounding Language in Graphics using Frame Semantics
Bob Coyne, Daniel Bauer and Owen Rambow

12:15-13:40 Lunch break

Thursday: June 23, 2011 (continued)

13:40-14:30 **Session 3**

(13:40-14:05)
Transition-based Semantic Role Labeling Using Predicate Argument Clustering
Jinho D. Choi and Martha Palmer

(14:05-14:30)
Using Grammar Rule Clusters for Semantic Relation Classification
Emily Jamison

14:30-15:30 **Panel**

- Timothy Baldwin, The University of Melbourne
- Eduard Hovy, University of Southern California
- Saif Mohammad, National Research Council Canada
- Sebastian Riedel, University of Massachusetts

15:30-16:00 Afternoon break

16:00-17:15 **Session 4**

(16:00-16:25)
Desperately Seeking Implicit Arguments in Text
Sara Tonelli and Rodolfo Delmonte

(16:25-16:50)
A Joint Model of Implicit Arguments for Nominal Predicates
Matthew Gerber, Joyce Chai and Robert Bart

(16:50-17:15)
Incorporating Coercive Constructions into a Verb Lexicon
Claire Bonial, Susan Windisch Brown, Jena D. Hwang, Christopher Parisien, Martha Palmer and Suzanne Stevenson

17:15-17:20 **Closing remarks**

Going Beyond Shallow Semantics
(invited talk)

Martha Palmer
University of Colorado at Boulder
Martha.Palmer@colorado.edu

Abstract

Shallow semantic analyzers, such as semantic role labeling and sense tagging, are increasing in accuracy and becoming commonplace. However, they only provide limited and local representations of local words and individual predicate-argument structures. This talk will address some of the current challenges in producing deeper, connected representations of eventualities. Available resources, such as VerbNet, FrameNet and TimeBank, that can assist in this process will also be discussed, as well as some of their limitations.

Speaker's Bio

Martha Palmer is a Full Professor at the University of Colorado with joint appointments in Linguistics and Computer Science and is an Institute of Cognitive Science Faculty Fellow. She recently won a Boulder Faculty Assembly 2010 Research Award. Beginning with her dissertation work at Edinburgh and her first job as a Research Scientist at Unisys, her research has been focused on trying to capture the meanings of words in representations that the computer can use to build up meanings of complex sentences and documents. These representations can in turn be used to improve the computer's ability to perform question answering, information retrieval, and machine translation. Current approaches rely on techniques for applying supervised machine learning algorithms, which use vast amounts of annotated training data. Therefore, she and her students, both at Colorado and previously at the University of Pennsylvania, are engaged in providing data with word sense tags and semantic role labels for English, Chinese, Arabic, and Hindi, funded by DARPA and NSF. They also use machine learning algorithms to develop automatic sense taggers and semantic role labelers, and to extract bilingual lexicons from parallel corpora. A more recent focus is the application of these methods to biomedical journal articles and clinical notes, funded by NIH. She is a co-editor for both the Journal of Natural Language Engineering and LiLT, Linguistic Issues in Language Technology. She is a past President of the Association for Computational Linguistics, past Chair of SIGLEX and SIGHAN, and is currently the Director of the 2011 Linguistics Institute to be held in Boulder, Colorado.

Customizing an Information Extraction System to a New Domain

Mihai Surdeanu, David McClosky, Mason R. Smith, Andrey Gusev, and Christopher D. Manning
Department of Computer Science
Stanford University
Stanford, CA 94305
{mihais,mcclosky,mrsmith,manning}@stanford.edu
agusev@cs.stanford.edu

Abstract

We introduce several ideas that improve the performance of supervised information extraction systems with a pipeline architecture, when they are customized for new domains. We show that: (a) a combination of a sequence tagger with a rule-based approach for entity mention extraction yields better performance for both entity and relation mention extraction; (b) improving the identification of syntactic heads of entity mentions helps relation extraction; and (c) a deterministic inference engine captures some of the joint domain structure, even when introduced as a post-processing step to a pipeline system. All in all, our contributions yield a 20% relative increase in F1 score in a domain significantly different from the domains used during the development of our information extraction system.

1 Introduction

Information extraction (IE) systems generally consist of multiple interdependent components, e.g., entity mentions predicted by an entity mention detection (EMD) model connected by relations via a relation mention detection (RMD) component (Yao et al., 2010; Roth and Yih, 2007; Surdeanu and Ciaramita, 2007). Figure 1 shows a sentence from a sports domain where both entity and relation mentions are annotated. When training data exists, the best performance in IE is generally obtained by supervised machine learning approaches. In this scenario, the typical approach for domain customization is apparently straightforward: simply retrain on data from the new domain (and potentially tune model parameters). In this paper we argue that, even when considerable training data is available, this is not sufficient to maximize performance. We apply several simple ideas that yield a significant performance boost, and can be implemented with minimal effort. In particular:

- We show that a combination of a conditional random field model (Lafferty et al., 2001) with a rule-based approach that is recall oriented yields better performance for EMD and for the downstream RMD component. The rule-based approach includes gazetteers, which have been shown to be important by Mikheev et al. (1999), among others.
- We improve the unification of the predicted semantic annotations with the syntactic analysis of the corresponding text, i.e., finding the syntactic head of a given semantic constituent. Since many features in an IE system depend on syntactic analysis, this leads to more consistent features and better extraction models.
- We add a simple inference engine that generates additional relation mentions based solely on the relation mentions extracted by the RMD model. This engine mitigates some of the limitations of a text-based RMD model, which cannot extract relations not explicitly stated in text.

We investigate these ideas using an IE system that performs recognition of entity mentions followed by extraction of binary relations between these mentions. We used as target a sports domain that is significantly different from the corpora previously used with this IE system. The target domain is also significantly different from the dataset used to train the

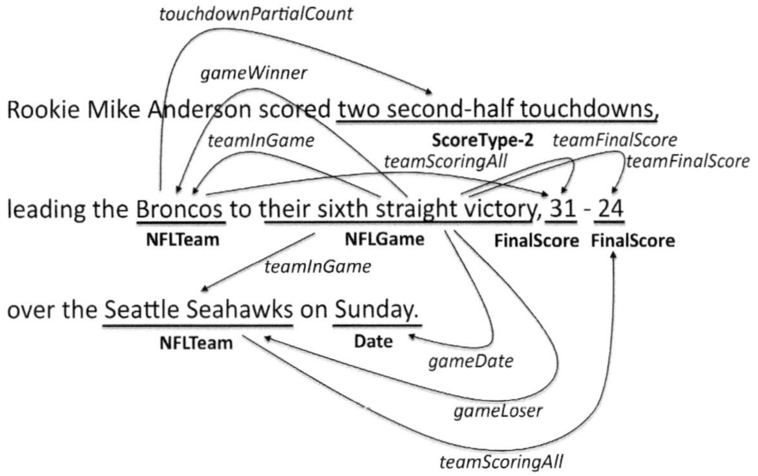

Figure 1: Sample sentence from the NFL domain. The domain contains entity mentions (underlined with entity types in bold) and binary relations between entity mentions (indicated by arrows; relation types are italicized).

supporting natural language processing tools (e.g., syntactic parser). Our investigation shows that, despite their simplicity, all our proposals help, yielding a 20% relative improvement in RMD F1 score.

The paper is organized as follows: Section 2 surveys related work. Section 3 describes the IE system used. We cover the target domain that serves as use case in this paper in Section 4. Section 5 introduces our ideas and evaluates their impact in the target domain. Finally, Section 6 concludes the paper.

2 Related Work

Other recent works have analyzed the robustness of information extraction systems. For example, Florian et al. (2010) observed that EMD systems perform badly on noisy inputs, e.g., automatic speech transcripts, and propose system combination (similar to our first proposal) to increase robustness in such scenarios. Ratinov and Roth (2009) also investigate design challenges for named entity recognition, and showed that other design choices, such as the representation of output labels and using features built on external knowledge, are more important than the learning model itself. These works are conceptually similar to our paper, but we propose several additional directions to improve robustness, and we investigate their impact in a complete IE system instead of just EMD.

Several of our lessons are drawn from the BioCreative challenge[1] and the BioNLP shared task (Kim et al., 2009). These tasks have shown the importance of high quality syntactic annotations and using heuristic fixes to correct systematic errors (Schuman and Bergler, 2006; Poon and Vanderwende, 2010, among others). Systems in the latter task have also shown the importance of high recall in the earlier stages of pipeline system.

[1] http://biocreative.sourceforge.net/

3 Description of the Generic IE System

We illustrate our proposed ideas using a simple IE system that implements a pipeline architecture: entity mention extraction followed by relation mention extraction. Note however that the domain customization discussion in Section 5 is independent of the system architecture or classifiers used for EMD and RMD, and we expect the proposed ideas to apply to other IE approaches as well.

We performed all pre-processing (tokenization, part-of-speech (POS) tagging) with the Stanford CoreNLP toolkit.[2] For EMD we used the Stanford named entity recognizer (Finkel et al., 2005). In all our experiments we used a generic set of features ("macro") and the IO notation[3] for entity mention labels (e.g., the labels for the tokens "over the Seattle Seahawks on Sunday" (from Figure 1) are encoded as "O O NFLTEAM NFLTEAM O DATE").

[2] http://nlp.stanford.edu/software/corenlp.shtml

[3] The IO notation facilitates faster inference than the IOB or IOB2 notations with minimal impact on performance, when there are fewer adjacent mentions with the same type.

Argument Features	– Head words of the two arguments and their combination – Entity mention labels of the two arguments and their combination
Syntactic Features	– Sequence of dependency labels in the dependency path linking the heads of the two arguments – Lemmas of all words in the dependency path – Syntactic path in the constituent parse tree between the largest constituents headed by the same words as the two arguments (similar to Gildea and Jurafsky (2002))
Surface Features	– Concatenation of POS tags between arguments – Binary indicators set to true if there is an entity mention with a given type between the two arguments

Table 1: Feature set used for RMD.

The RMD model was built from scratch as a multi-class classifier that extracts binary relations between entity mentions in the same sentence. During training, known relation mentions become positive examples for the corresponding label and all other possible combinations between entity mentions in the same sentence become negative examples. We used a multiclass logistic regression classifier with L2 regularization. Our feature set is taken from (Yao et al., 2010; Mintz et al., 2009; Roth and Yih, 2007; Surdeanu and Ciaramita, 2007) and models the relation arguments, the surface distance between the relation arguments, and the syntactic path between the two arguments, using both constituency and dependency representations. For syntactic information, we used the Stanford parser (Klein and Manning, 2003) and the Stanford dependency representation (de Marneffe et al., 2006).

For RMD, we implemented an additive feature selection algorithm similar to the one in (Surdeanu et al., 2008), which iteratively adds the feature with the highest improvement in F1 score to the current feature set, until no improvement is seen. The algorithm was configured to select features that yielded the best combined performance on the dataset from Roth and Yih (2007) and the training partition of ACE 2007.[4] We used ten-fold cross validation on both datasets. We decided to use a standard F1 score to evaluate RMD performance rather than the more complex ACE score because we believe that the former is more interpretable. We used gold entity mentions for the feature selection process. Table 1 summarizes the final set of features selected.

Documents	Words	Entity Mentions	Relation Mentions
110	70,119	2,188	1,629

Table 2: Summary statistics of the NFL corpus, after our conversion to binary relations.

Despite its simplicity, our approach achieves comparable performance with other state-of-the-art results reported on these datasets (Roth and Yih, 2007; Surdeanu and Ciaramita, 2007). For example, Surdeanu and Ciaramita report a RMD F1 score of 59.4 for ACE relation types (i.e., ignoring subtypes) when gold entity mentions are used. Under the same conditions, our RMD model obtains a F1 score of 59.2.

4 Description of the Target Domain

In this paper we report results on the "Machine Reading NFL Scoring" corpus.[5] This corpus was developed by LDC for the DARPA Machine Reading project. The corpus contains 110 newswire articles on National Football League (NFL) games. The annotations cover game information, such as participating teams, winners and losers, partial (e.g., a single touchdown or three field goals) and final scores. Most of the annotated relations in the original corpus are binary (e.g. GAMEDATE(NFLGAME, DATE)) but some are n-ary relations or include other attributes in addition of the relation type. We reduce these to annotations compatible with our RMD approach as follows:

- We concatenate the cardinality of each scoring event (i.e. how many scoring events are being talked about) to the corresponding SCORETYPE entity label. Thus SCORETYPE-2 indicates that there were two of a given type of scoring event (touchdown, field goal, etc.). This operation is necessary because the cardinality of scoring events is originally annotated as an additional attribute of the SCORETYPE

[4] LDC catalog numbers LDC2006E54 and LDC2007E11

[5] LDC catalog number LDC2009E112

Entity Mentions	Correct	Predicted	Actual	P	R	F1
Date	141	190	174	74.2	81.0	77.5
FinalScore	299	328	347	91.2	86.2	88.6
NFLGame	71	109	147	65.1	48.3	55.5
NFLPlayoffGame	8	25	38	32.0	21.1	25.4
NFLTeam	651	836	818	77.9	79.6	78.7
ScoreType-1	329	479	525	68.7	62.7	65.5
ScoreType-2	49	68	79	72.1	62.0	66.7
ScoreType-3	17	26	36	65.4	47.2	54.8
ScoreType-4	6	11	14	54.5	42.9	48.0
Total	1571	2076	2188	75.7	71.8	73.7

Relation Mentions	Correct	Predicted	Actual	P	R	F1
fieldGoalPartialCount	33	41	101	80.5	32.7	46.5
gameDate	32	36	115	88.9	27.8	42.4
gameLoser	22	44	124	50.0	17.7	26.2
gameWinner	6	15	123	40.0	4.9	8.7
teamFinalScore	95	101	232	94.1	40.9	57.1
teamInGame	49	105	257	46.7	19.1	27.1
teamScoringAll	202	232	321	87.1	62.9	73.1
touchDownPartialCount	156	191	322	81.7	48.4	60.8
Total	595	766	1629	77.7	36.5	49.7

Table 3: Baseline results: stock system without any domain customization. Correct/Predicted/Actual indicate the number of mentions (entities or relations) that are correctly predicted/predicted/gold. P/R/F1 indicate precision/recall/F1 scores for the corresponding label.

entity and our EMD approach does not model mention attributes.

- We split all n-ary relations into several new binary relations. For example, the original TEAMFINALSCORE(NFLTEAM, NFLGAME, FINALSCORE) relation is split into three binary relations: TEAMSCORINGALL(NFLTEAM, FINALSCORE), TEAMINGAME(NFLGAME, NFLTEAM), and TEAMFINALSCORE(NFLGAME, FINALSCORE).

Figure 1 shows an example annotated sentence after the above conversion and Table 2 lists the corpus summary statistics for the new binary relations.

The purpose behind this corpus is to encourage the development of systems that answer structured queries that go beyond the functionality of information retrieval engines, e.g.:

> "For each NFL game, identify the winning and losing teams and each team's final score in the game."

> "For each team losing to the Green Bay Packers, tell us the losing team and the number of points they scored."[6]

5 Domain Customization

Table 3 lists the results of the generic IE system described in Section 3 on the NFL domain. Throughout this paper we will report results using ten-fold cross-validation on all 110 documents in the corpus.[7] We consider an entity mention as correct if both its boundaries and label match exactly the gold mention. We consider a relation mention correct if both its arguments and label match the gold relation mention. For RMD, we report results using the actual mentions predicted by our EMD model (instead of using gold entity mentions for RMD). For clarity, we do not show in the tables some labels that are highly uncommon in the data (e.g., SCORETYPE-5 appears only four times in the entire corpus); but the "Total" results include all entity and relation mentions.

Table 3 shows that the stock IE system obtains an

[6]These queries would be written in a formal language but are presented here in English for clarity.

[7]Generally, we do not condone reporting results using cross-validation because it may be a recipe for over-fitting on the corresponding corpus. However, all our domain customization ideas were developed using outside world and domain knowledge and were not tuned on this data, so we believe that there is minimal over-fitting in this case.

Entity Mentions	P	R	F1
Date	74.2	81.0	77.5
FinalScore	91.3	87.3	89.2
NFLGame	61.2	48.3	54.0
NFLPlayoffGame	33.3	21.1	25.8
NFLTeam	77.9	81.3	79.5
ScoreType-1	68.8	62.3	65.4
ScoreType-2	72.1	62.0	66.7
ScoreType-3	65.4	47.2	54.8
ScoreType-4	54.5	42.9	48.0
Total	75.6	72.5	74.0

Relation Mentions	P	R	F1
fieldGoalPartialCount	78.0	31.7	45.1
gameDate	91.4	27.8	42.7
gameLoser	50.0	18.5	27.1
gameWinner	40.0	4.9	8.7
teamFinalScore	94.1	40.9	57.1
teamInGame	45.9	19.5	27.3
teamScoringAll	87.0	64.8	74.3
touchDownPartialCount	82.4	49.4	61.7
Total	77.6	37.1	50.2

Table 4: Performance after gazetteer-based features were added to the EMD model.

Entity Mentions	P	R	F1
Date	74.2	81.0	77.5
FinalScore	91.3	87.3	89.2
NFLGame	61.2	48.3	54.0
NFLPlayoffGame	33.3	21.1	25.8
NFLTeam	71.4	96.9	82.3
ScoreType-1	68.8	62.3	65.4
ScoreType-2	72.1	62.0	66.7
ScoreType-3	65.4	47.2	54.8
ScoreType-4	54.5	42.9	48.0
Total	72.8	78.4	75.5

Relation Mentions	P	R	F1
fieldGoalPartialCount	81.2	38.6	52.3
gameDate	93.9	27.0	41.9
gameLoser	51.1	19.4	28.1
gameWinner	38.9	5.7	9.9
teamFinalScore	94.1	40.9	57.1
teamInGame	47.4	24.5	32.3
teamScoringAll	87.0	68.8	76.9
touchDownPartialCount	81.6	56.5	66.8
Total	77.2	40.6	53.2

Table 5: Performance after gazetteer-based features were added to the EMD model, and NFLTeam entity mentions were extracted using the rule-based model rather than classification.

EMD F1 score of 73.7 and a RMD F1 score of 49.7. These are respectable results, in line with state-of-the-art results in other domains.[8] However, there are some obvious areas for improvement. For example, the score for a few relations (e.g., GAMELOSER and GAMEWINNER) is quite low. This is caused by the fact that these relations are often not explicitly stated in text but rather implied (e.g., based on team scores). Furthermore, the low recall of entity types that are crucial for all relations (e.g., NFLTEAM and NFLGAME) negatively impacts the overall recall of RMD.

5.1 Combining a Rule-based Model with Conditional Random Fields for EMD

A straightforward way to improve EMD performance is to construct domain-specific gazetteers and include gazetteer-based features in the model. We constructed a NFL-specific gazetteer as follows: (a) we included all 32 NFL team names; (b) we built a lexicon for NFLGame nouns and verbs that included game types (e.g., "semi-final", "quarter-final") and typical game descriptors. The game descriptors were manually bootstrapped from three seed words ("victory", "loss", "game") using Dekang Lin's dependency-based thesaurus.[9] This process added other relevant game descriptors such as "triumph", "defeat", etc. All in all, our gazetteer includes 32 team names and 50 game descriptors. The gazetteer was built in less than four person hours.

We added features to our EMD model to indicate if a sequence of words matches a gazetteer entry, allowing approximate matches (e.g., "Cowboys" matches "Dallas Cowboys"). Table 4 lists the results after this change. The improvements are modest: 0.3 for both EMD and RMD, caused by a 0.8 improvement for NFLTEAM. The score for NFLGAME suffers a loss of 1.5 F1 points, probably caused by the fact that our NFLGAME gazetteer is incomplete.

These results are somewhat disappointing: even though our gazetteer contains an exhaustive list of NFL team names, the EMD recall for NFLTEAM is still relatively low. This happens because city

[8] As a comparison, the best RMD system in ACE 2007 obtained an ACE score of less than 35%, even though the ACE score gives credit for approximate matches of entity mention boundaries (Surdeanu and Ciaramita, 2007).

[9] http://webdocs.cs.ualberta.ca/~lindek/Downloads/sim.tgz

names that are not references to team names are relatively common in this corpus, and the CRF model favors the generic city name interpretation. However, since the goal is to answer structured queries over the extracted relations, we would prefer a model that favors recall for EMD, to avoid losing candidates for RMD. While this can be achieved in different ways (Minkov et al., 2006), in this paper we implement a very simple approach: we recognize NFLTEAM mentions with a rule-based system that extracts all token sequences that begin, end, or are equal to a known team name. For example, "Green Bay" and "Packers" are marked as team mentions, but not "Bay". Note that this approach is prone to introducing false positives, e.g., "Green" in the above example. For all other entity types we use the CRF model with gazetteer-based features. Table 5 lists the results for this model combination. The table shows that the RMD performance is improved by 3 F1 points. The F1 score for NFLTEAM mentions is also improved by 3 points, due to a significant increase in recall (from 81% to 97%).

Of course, this simple idea works only for entity types with low ambiguity. In fact, it does not improve results if we apply it to NFLGAME or SCORETYPE-*. However, low ambiguity entities are common in many domains (e.g., medical). In such domains, our approach offers a straightforward way to address potential recall errors of a machine learned model.

5.2 Improving Head Identification for Entity Mentions

Table 1 indicates that most RMD features (e.g., lexical information on arguments, dependency paths between arguments) depend on the syntactic heads of entity mentions. This observation applies to other natural language processing (NLP) tasks as well, e.g., semantic role labeling or coreference resolution (Gildea and Jurafsky, 2002; Haghighi and Klein, 2009). It is thus crucial that syntactic heads of mentions be correctly identified. Originally we employed a common heuristic: we first try to find a constituent with the exact same span as the given entity mention in the parse tree of the entire sentence, and extract its head. If no such constituent exists, we parse only the text corresponding to the mention and return the head of the generated tree (Haghighi

Entity Mentions	P	R	F1
Date	69.5	75.9	72.5
FinalScore	90.9	88.8	89.8
NFLGame	60.5	51.0	55.4
NFLPlayoffGame	37.0	26.3	30.8
NFLTeam	72.4	98.3	83.4
ScoreType-1	69.7	62.1	65.7
ScoreType-2	76.9	63.3	69.4
ScoreType-3	64.3	50.0	56.3
ScoreType-4	72.7	57.1	64.0
Total	73.2	79.2	76.1

Relation Mentions	P	R	F1
fieldGoalPartialCount	81.2	55.4	65.9
gameDate	93.9	27.0	41.9
gameLoser	51.2	17.7	26.3
gameWinner	50.0	8.9	15.2
teamFinalScore	96.5	47.4	63.6
teamInGame	48.3	33.5	39.5
teamScoringAll	86.7	72.9	79.2
touchDownPartialCount	89.1	61.2	72.6
Total	78.5	45.9	57.9

Table 6: Performance with the improved syntactic head identification rules.

and Klein, 2009). Here we argue that the last step of this heuristic is flawed: since most parsers are heavily context dependent, they are likely to not parse correctly arbitrarily short text fragments. For example, the Stanford parser generates the incorrect parse tree:

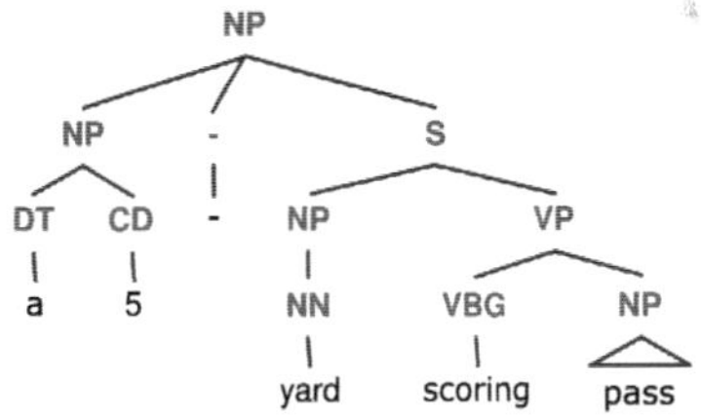

The syntactic head is "5" for the mention "a 5-yard scoring pass" instead of "pass."[10] This problem is exacerbated out of domain, where the parse tree of the entire sentence is likely to be incorrect, which will often trigger the parsing of the isolated mention text. For example, in the NFL domain, more than 25% of entity mentions cannot be matched to a constituent in the parse tree of the corresponding sentence.

[10]We tokenize around dashes in this domain because scores are often dash separated. However, this mention is incorrectly parsed even when "5-yard" is a single token.

```
teamFinalScore(G, S) :-  teamInGame(T, G), teamScoringAll(T, S).
teamFinalScore(G, S) :-  gameWinner(T, G), teamScoringAll(T, S).
teamFinalScore(G, S) :-  gameLoser(T, G), teamScoringAll(T, S).
    teamInGame(G, T) :-  teamScoringAll(T, S), teamFinalScore(G, S).
   gameWinner(G, T1) :-  teamInGame(G, T1), teamInGame(G, T2),
                         teamFinalScore(G, S1), teamFinalScore(G, S2),
                         teamScoringAll(T1, S1), teamScoringAll(T2, S2),
                         greaterThan(S1, S2).
    gameLoser(G, T1) :-  teamInGame(G, T1), teamInGame(G, T2),
                         teamFinalScore(G, S1), teamFinalScore(G, S2),
                         teamScoringAll(T1, S1), teamScoringAll(T2, S2),
                         lessThan(S1, S2).
```

Table 7: Deterministic inference rules for the NFL domain as first-order Horn clauses. `G`, `T`, and `S` indicate game, team, and score variables.

In this work, we propose several simple heuristics that improve the parsing of isolated mention texts:

- We append "It was " to the beginning of the text to be parsed. Since entity mentions are noun phrases (NP), the new text is guaranteed to be a coherent sentence. A similar heuristic was used by Moldovan and Rus for the parsing of WordNet glosses (2001).
- Because dashes are uncommon in the Penn Treebank, we remove them from the text before parsing.
- We guide the Stanford parser such that the final tree contains a constituent with the same span as the mention text.[11]

After implementing these heuristics, the Stanford parser correctly parses the mention in the above example as a NP headed by "pass". Table 6 lists the overall extraction scores after deploying these heuristics. The table shows that the RMD F1 score is a considerable 4.7 points higher than before this change (Table 5).

5.3 Deterministic Inference for RMD

Figure 1 underlines the fact that relations in the NFL domain are highly inter-dependent. This is a common occurrence in many extraction tasks and domains (Poon and Vanderwende, 2010; Carlson et al., 2010). The typical way to address these situations is to jointly model these relations, e.g., using Markov logic networks (MLN) (Poon and Vanderwende, 2010). However, this implies a complete redesign of the corresponding IE system, which would essentially ignore all the effort behind existing pipeline systems.

[11]This is supported by the parser API.

Relation Mentions	P	R	F1
fieldGoalPartialCount	81.2	55.4	65.9
gameDate	93.9	27.0	41.9
gameLoser	45.9	27.4	34.3
gameWinner	45.6	25.2	32.5
teamFinalScore	96.5	47.4	63.6
teamInGame	48.1	44.7	46.4
teamScoringAll	86.7	72.9	79.2
touchDownPartialCount	89.1	61.2	72.6
Total	74.2	49.6	59.5

Table 8: Performance after adding deterministic inference. The EMD scores are not affected by this change, so they are not listed here.

In this work, we propose a simple method that captures some of the joint domain structure independently of the IE architecture and the EMD and RMD models. We add a deterministic inference component that generates new relation mentions based on the data already extracted by the pipeline model. Table 7 lists the rules of this inference component that were developed for the NFL domain. These rules are domain-dependent, but they are quite simple: the first four rules implement transitive-closure rules for relation mentions centered around the same NFLGAME mention; the last two add domain knowledge that is not captured by the text extractors, e.g., the game winner is the team with the higher score. Table 8, which lists the RMD scores after inference, indicates that the inference component is responsible for an increase of approximately 2 F1 points, caused by a recall boost of approximately 4%.

Table 9 lists the results of a post-hoc experiment, where we removed several relation types from the RMD classifier (the ones predicted with poor performance) and let the deterministic inference component generate them instead. This experiment shows

	Without Inference			With Inference		
	P	R	F1	P	R	F1
Skip gameWinner, gameLoser	**78.6**	45.6	57.7	**75.1**	48.4	58.8
Skip teamInGame	77.0	43.6	55.7	71.7	49.4	58.5
Skip teamInGame, teamFinalScore	74.5	37.1	49.6	70.9	47.6	56.9
Skip nothing	78.5	**45.9**	**57.9**	74.2	**49.6**	**59.5**

Table 9: Analysis of different combination strategies between the RMD classifier and inference: the RMD model skips the relation types listed in the first column; the inference component generates all relation types. The other columns show relation mention scores under the various configurations.

	EMD	RMD
	F1	F1
Baseline	73.7	49.7
+ gazetteer features	74.0	50.2
+ rule-based model for NFLTeam	75.5	53.2
+ improved head identification	**76.1**	57.9
+ inference	**76.1**	**59.5**

Table 10: Summary of domain customization results.

that inference helps in all configurations, and, most importantly, it is robust: even though the RMD score without inference decreases by up to 8 F1 points as relations are removed, the score after inference varies by less than 3 F1 points (from 56.9 to 59.5 F1). This proves that deterministic inference is capable of generating relation mentions that are either missed or cannot be modeled by the RMD classifier.

Finally, Table 10 summarizes the experiments presented in this paper. It is clear that, despite their simplicity, all our proposed ideas help. All in all, our contributions yielded an improvement of 9.8 F1 points (approximately 20% relative) over the stock IE system without these changes. Our best IE system was used in a blind evaluation within the Machine Reading project. In this evaluation, systems were required to answer 50 queries similar to the examples in Section 4 and were evaluated on the correctness of the individual facts extracted. Note that this evaluation is more complex than the experiments reported until now, because the corresponding IE system requires additional components, e.g., the normalization of all DATE mentions and event coreference (i.e., are two different game mentions referring to the same real-world game?). For this evaluation, we used an internal script for date normalization and we did not implement event coreference. This system was evaluated at 46.7 F1 (53.7 precision and 41.2 recall), a performance that was approximately 80% of the F1 score obtained by human annotators. This further highlights that strong IE performance can be obtained with simple models.

6 Conclusions

This paper introduces a series of simple ideas that improve the performance of IE systems when they are customized to new domains. We evaluated our contributions on a sports domain (NFL game summaries) that is significantly different from the domains used to develop our IE system or the language processors used by our system.

Our analysis revealed several interesting and non-obvious facts. First, we showed that accurate identification of syntactic heads of entity mentions, which has received little attention in IE literature, is crucial for good performance. Second, we showed that a deterministic inference component captures some of the joint domain structure, even when the underlying system follows a pipeline architecture. Lastly, we introduced a simple way to tune precision and recall by combining our entity mention extractor with a rule-based system. Overall, our contributions yielded a 20% improvement in the F1 score for relation mention extraction.

We believe that our contributions are model independent and some, e.g., the better head identification, even task independent. Some of our ideas require domain knowledge, but they are all very simple to implement. We thus expect them to impact other problems as well, e.g., coreference resolution, semantic role labeling.

Acknowledgments

We thank the reviewers for their detailed comments.

This material is based upon work supported by the Air Force Research Laboratory (AFRL) under prime contract no. FA8750-09-C-0181. Any opinions, findings, and conclusion or recommendations expressed in this material are those of the authors and do not necessarily reflect the view of the Air Force Research Laboratory (AFRL).

References

Andrew Carlson, Justin Betteridge, Richard C. Wang, Estevam R. Hruschka Jr., and Tom M. Mitchell. 2010. Coupled semi-supervised learning for information extraction. In *Proceedings of the Third ACM International Conference on Web Search and Data Mining (WSDM)*.

Marie-Catherine de Marneffe, Bill MacCartney, and Christopher D. Manning. 2006. Generating typed dependency parses from phrase structure parses. In *LREC*.

Jenny Rose Finkel, Trond Grenager, and Christopher Manning. 2005. Incorporating non-local information into information extraction systems by gibbs sampling. In *Proceedings of the 43nd Annual Meeting of the Association for Computational Linguistics (ACL 2005)*.

Radu Florian, John Pitrelli, Salim Roukos, and Imed Zitouni. 2010. Improving mention detection robustness to noisy input. In *Proc. of Empirical Methods in Natural Language Processing (EMNLP)*.

Daniel Gildea and Daniel Jurafsky. 2002. Automatic labeling of semantic roles. *Computational Linguistics*, 28(3).

Aria Haghighi and Dan Klein. 2009. Simple coreference resolution with rich syntactic and semantic features. In *Proc. of Empirical Methods in Natural Language Processing (EMNLP)*.

Jin-Dong Kim, Tomoko Ohta, Sampo Pyysalo, Yoshinobu Kano, and Jun'ichi Tsujii. 2009. Overview of BioNLP'09 shared task on event extraction. In *Proceedings of the Workshop on BioNLP: Shared Task*, pages 1–9. Association for Computational Linguistics.

Dan Klein and Christopher D. Manning. 2003. Accurate unlexicalized parsing. In *Proceedings of the 41st Meeting of the Association for Computational Linguistics*.

John Lafferty, Andrew McCallum, and Fernando Pereira. 2001. Conditional Random Fields: Probabilistic models for segmenting and labeling sequence data. In *Proc. of the International Conference on Machine Learning (ICML)*.

Andrei Mikheev, Marc Moens, and Claire Grover. 1999. Named entity recognition without gazetteers. In *EACL*, pages 1–8.

Einat Minkov, Richard C. Wang, Anthony Tomasic, and William W. Cohen. 2006. Ner systems that suit user's preferences: Adjusting the recall-precision trade-off for entity extraction. In *Proc. of HLT/NAACL*.

M. Mintz, S. Bills, R. Snow, and D. Jurafsky. 2009. Distant supervision for relation extraction without labeled data. In *Proc. of the Conference of the Association for Computational Linguistics (ACL-IJCNLP)*.

Dan I. Moldovan and Vasile Rus. 2001. Logic form transformation of wordnet and its applicability to question answering. In *Proceedings of the Annual Meeting of the Association for Computational Linguistics*.

Hoifung Poon and Lucy Vanderwende. 2010. Joint inference for knowledge extraction from biomedical literature. In *Proceedings of the North American Chapter of the Association for Computational Linguistics - Human Language Technologies Conference (NAACL-HLT)*.

Lev Ratinov and Dan Roth. 2009. Design challenges and misconceptions in named entity recognition. In *Proc. of the Annual Conference on Computational Natural Language Learning (CoNLL)*.

D. Roth and W. Yih. 2007. Global inference for entity and relation identification via a linear programming formulation. In *Introduction to Statistical Relational Learning*. MIT Press.

Jonathan Schuman and Sabine Bergler. 2006. Postnominal prepositional phrase attachment in proteomics. In *Proceedings of the HLT-NAACL BioNLP Workshop on Linking Natural Language and Biology*, pages 82–89. Association for Computational Linguistics, June.

Mihai Surdeanu and Massimiliano Ciaramita. 2007. Robust information extraction with perceptrons. In *Proceedings of the NIST 2007 Automatic Content Extraction Workshop (ACE07)*.

Mihai Surdeanu, Massimiliano Ciaramita, and Hugo Zaragoza. 2008. Learning to rank answers on large online qa collections. In *Proceedings of the 46th Annual Meeting of the Association for Computational Linguistics (ACL 2008)*.

Limin Yao, Sebastian Riedel, and Andrew McCallum. 2010. Collective cross-document relation extraction without labelled data. In *Proc. of Empirical Methods in Natural Language Processing (EMNLP)*.

Extraction of Semantic Word Relations in Turkish from Dictionary Definitions

Şerbetçi Ayşe
Computer Engineering Department
Fatih University
34500
Buyukcekmece, Istanbul, Turkey
aserbetci@fatih.edu.tr

Orhan Zeynep
Computer Engineering Department
Fatih University
34500
Buyukcekmece, Istanbul, Turkey
zorhan@fatih.edu.tr

Pehlivan İlknur
firstnoor@gmail.com

Abstract

Many recent studies have been dedicated to the extraction of semantic connections between words. Using such information at semantic level is likely to improve the performance of Natural Language Processing (NLP) systems, such as text categorization, question answering, information extraction, etc. The scarcity of such resources in Turkish, obstructs new improvements. There are many examples of semantic networks for English and other widely-used languages to lead the way for studies in Turkish. In this study, developing a semantic network for Turkish is aimed by using structural and string patterns in a dictionary. The results are promising, so that approximately two relations can be extracted from 3 definitions. The overall accuracy is 86% if we consider the correct sense assignment, 94% without considering word sense disambiguation.

1 Introduction

Nowadays, the internet is the primary media, people use for communicating with each other and sharing their ideas with the rest of the world. Therefore, a massive amount of data is available but it is not understandable to computers. Wide usage of the web brings some requirements to make this data more beneficial for people. Understanding text from a foreign language or accessing relevant ones among millions of documents has become crucially important. However, due to the large size of data, it is very difficult for human to maintain these tasks without rapid computer processing. Automatic text summarization, information extraction and text categorization are all important NLP areas, which aim to help humans benefit from computer systems to perform these tasks.

The process of obtaining robust computer systems capable of handling these tasks involves supporting machines with semantic knowledge. The type of necessary knowledge depends on the target system. Nevertheless, the information of what kinds of relations exist between the words can be very useful for many purposes especially for NLP applications. Starting with the WordNet project in 1985, semantic networks or lexical databases have been among the important study areas in NLP up to the present. WordNet project (http://wordnet.princeton.edu/wordnet/download/).

Obtaining a semantic network for Turkish language is the goal of this study. Since this study is an initial step of developing a semantic network in Turkish, basic relationship of hyponymy and synonymy are primarily handled. For this purpose, the investigation of dictionary definitions and the morphological richness of Turkish language are utilized. Different types of relationships are shown in Table 1. Since these relationships are very basic, they are likely to be used in various kinds of NLP tasks.

Various patterns are extracted from dictionary by using both syntax and string features of the definitions. Each definition represents particular sense of a word, so they can be considered as different words. For more accurate semantic analysis, the connection between words should be established between appropriate senses of the words. To be more concrete, an example can be given on the semantically ambiguous word as; yüz 'face' or 'hundred'. When a has-a relation is detected between the words vücut 'body' and yüz, the appropriate sense for yüz should be selected as 'face', instead of 'hundred'.

Relationship	Example
Is-a(hyponymy)	flower-plant
Synonym-of	initial-first
Antonym-of	quick-slow
Member-of	academician-academy
Amount-of	kg-weight
Group-of	forest-tree
Has-a	office-computer

Table 1: Basic word relationships

The rest of the paper is organized as follows: Section 2 discusses the previous work in this field. Section 3 explains the implementation methods, details and approaches to some NLP problems, like morphology or word sense ambiguity. This section also gives some statistics about the results. The future work to be performed for both improving and extending the network is also discussed in this section. Section 4 evaluates the overall system.

2 Previous Work

Cyc (http://www.opencyc.org) project is one of the first attempts of obtaining computer accessible world knowledge. Many other studies have been performed for constructing large lexical databases or semantic networks by extracting the semantic connections between words.

In fact, both the number and types of the possible relationships are not clearly identified in this area. However, there are some widely accepted basic relationships, which can be considered as the backbone of semantic networks. No matter which method is followed for extracting these connections, most of the studies including WordNet (Miller, 1995; Fellbaum, 1998) and ConceptNet(Havasi et al., 2007) are based on this set of specific relationships such as hyponymy, synonymy, meronymy etc. These are the most basic but also the most informative ones among the common relation types.

Some manual work has been performed at the beginning for constructing this kind of semantic networks, including but not limited with Wordnet. Nowadays, however, semi or fully automatic systems capable of performing these processes are worked on. Different methods have been used from collecting online data to corpus analysis and from defining syntactical rules to string patterns.

ConceptNet collects its data from Open Mind Common Sense Project (http://commons.media.mit.edu/en/), which is a web-based collaboration (Havasi et al., 2007). Over 15,000 authors enter sentences to contribute to the project. Users can answer questions via the web interface, which aim to fill the gaps in the project. However, in the study of Nakov and Hearts (2008), the whole web is treated like a corpus and the occurrences of the noun pairs together are converted into feature vectors to perform a classification for semantic relations.

There are various methods under the subject of string or structural patterns that represent specific semantic relations. Barriere(1997) investigates some syntactical rules in her study and matches the dictionary definitions to these rules for figuring out the relations. Also, in some languages in which prepositions are used frequently, some relations can be extracted depending on the prepositions, like in the study of Celli and Nessim (2009).

In addition, there are some studies which aim to extract some patterns for each relation for the purpose of finding new instances.

Turney's study (2006) is a good example, which uses a corpus based method for finding high quality patterns. It searches the noun pairs through the corpus to extract some row patterns. The patterns are ranked by a ranking algorithm in order to determine the most qualified patterns for the further steps. Espresso (Pantel and Pennacchiotti, 2006) is also concerned in finding patterns to represent relations. It starts with a few reliable seed of relations and iteratively learns the surface patterns in a given corpus.

There is a lot of work to be done for Turkish in this area. Except one project (Bilgin et al., 2004), which was performed and limited within the scope of BalkaNet project, there is no significant work in this area for Turkish.

BalkaNet project is valuable in the sense of being one of the first attempts for developing Turkish Wordnet. It differs from our study in its methodology, which involves translation of basic concepts in EuroWordNet and then using some string patterns to extend the network. In addition, target relationships and obtained results are quite different and will be handled in the following sections.

Another work (Önder, 2009) which aimed to extract the relations from dictionary definitions by using string patterns but was not completed, constructs the basics of our study.

3 Experimental Setup

In this section, the implementation process is discussed in the following order of sub topics:

- Data
- Morphological features of Turkish
- Extracted patterns
- Morphological analysis and disambiguation
- Word sense disambiguation
- Stop word removal
- Results

Using a dictionary can ease the process of extracting semantic relations in a language in many aspects. First of all, every word occurs in the dictionary at least once, hence the probability of missing a word decreases. Secondly, it consists of definitions of the words, which are relatively informative. Lastly, the sentences in a dictionary are generally simple and similar to each other. Therefore, they generally follow a set of syntactic patterns. This enables to perform easy detection of relations.

For all the reasons listed above, a dictionary of Turkish Language Association (TLA) is used in this study. There are 63110 words and 88268 senses in this dictionary. This concludes that nearly 25000 of the words are ambiguous. In Table 2, the distributions of these words among the most frequent parts of speech are given.

The first step is investigating the dictionary definitions manually in order to explore some patterns which are likely to keep a particular semantic relation inside. The patterns should be general enough for obtaining a reasonable recall. In addition, they should be specific enough not to cause low precision. After a rough analysis, the dictionary is scanned for some row patterns to evaluate the results in terms of both accuracy and comprehensiveness. According to the results, either patterns are reorganized or some additional features are determined to be used for increasing the number of matches and decreasing the error rate. Different kinds of features in the dictionary definitions and the words being explained are used. Morphological structures, noun clauses, clue words and the order of the words in the sentence are the examples of these features.

Part of Speech	Number
Noun	56400
Adjective	14554
Adverb	3011
Pronoun	104
Verb	11408

Table 2: The distributions of words in TLA dictionary

Turkish is an agglutinative language which results in a rich but rather complex morphological structure. Thus, the words do keep a very important part of the sense. They can be converted from one part of speech into another by adding derivational suffixes. For example, from the verb gelmek 'to come' the adjective gelen 'the one who comes' can be derived. This feature of Turkish constructs the most important effect of increasing the number of matches between patterns and definitions. In addition, indefinite noun phrases are detected with the help of morphological analysis and lots of relations are extracted as a result. These are only a few examples of where morphology is used when extracting the relations.

Some clue words in the definitions are also searched for. In dictionaries, some similar words are explained by using the same words and they can represent some specific relations. To be more concrete, the adjectives that represent the opposite of another adjective can be considered. These types of words are usually defined by using the words olmayan 'not' and karşıtı 'opposite of'. For example, in the definition of the word fantasik 'fantastic' there exists the phrase gerçek olmayan 'not real'. An antonymy relation can be established between the word fantastic 'fantastic' and gerçek 'real' as a result. For some other types of relations, different words are detected and handled. For example, for member-of relation, sınıfından 'from the class of'; for is-a relation, türü 'type of' are selected.

Additionally, noun clauses, which are defined in the dictionary, are investigated. Most of the time a noun phrase represents an 'is-a' relation. The word balık 'fish' and kılıç balığı 'sword fish' are both in the dictionary and kılıç balığı 'sword fish' is a noun phrase that has balık 'fish' in it. It is obvious that there is a connection between the words kılıç balığı 'sword fish' and balık 'fish'.

Various patterns are obtained by using at least one of the above features. The obtained patterns for each type of relation are shown in Table 3. When analyzing the table, the representatives to be considered are as follows: X and Y are used for representing the words being connected to each other, *punc* represents one of the specified punctuations like comma or full stop, w* represents zero or more sequential words, $w*_{no\_punct}$ represents zero or more sequential words without any punctuation inside, w_x is a word which keeps a specific part of speech x, depending on the pattern.

The extracted relations for the provided word definitions are not limited with those mentioned in the table. If possible, two or more relations can be extracted from a single definition. For instance, besides the 'member-of' relation between çakal 'jackal' and etoburlar 'carnivora', a 'kind-of' relation is extracted also for çakal 'jackal' with hayvan 'animal', since the definition matches with the fourth pattern of 'kind-of' relation. Although only the relation between pinhan 'latent' and saklı 'hidden' is given, another synonymy relation is also obtained from this pattern between pinhan 'latent' and gizli 'ulterior'.

The morphological structures of the words are obtained by using Zemberek project (http://code.google.com/p/zemberek), which is an open source morphological analyzer for Turkish. The analysis result of the word atan 'be assigned' or 'your ancestor' or 'the one who throws' is displayed with Figure 1.

The morphological ambiguity is handled with two different methods. Firstly, as a pre-processing step, some suffixes are determined, which cannot occur in the dictionary, such as time suffixes. The analyses are pruned from those results that include one or more of these suffixes. Secondly, according to the pattern requirements, the convenient result is selected as the correct one. For example, if a word is required to have a particular chain of suffixes, the first result providing this necessity is selected. If there is no assumption, the first result is selected by default.

The relations are established between the exact senses of the words in order to obtain a reliable network. Therefore, word sense disambiguation should also be performed. One of the words is not ambiguous, since one of its particular senses (definition) is already being handled for most of the relations. On the other hand, for the purpose of determining the correct sense of the remaining word, simplified Lesk algorithm is used(Lesk, 1986). Simplified Lesk algorithm benefits from the similarity measurements between each sense of the ambiguous word and the concept. The algorithm is given in Figure 2 and the details are provided in the http://en.wikipedia.org/wiki/Lesk_algorithm.

In order to obtain more accurate results, stemming and stop word removal is applied for both relation extraction and word sense disambiguation. A connection can be established only if both of the words are not stop words. Stop words are dictionary specific and obtained by counting the occurrences of word stems in the dictionary. Not all frequent stems are assumed to be stop words but the useless ones among the all stems whose occurrences are above an upper limit are ignored. There are 22 stop words specified, including için 'for', başka 'another' and en 'the most'.

The system was evaluated by manual calculation of the accuracy. Equal number of samples is chosen randomly from each pattern. Two types of accuracy were obtained, which are with and without consideration of correct sense assignment.

The obtained results are given in Table 4. The first accuracy column represents the accuracy percentage by considering whether the correct sense could be matched or not. The second column ignores the senses and evaluates the results in terms of the correct word relation only.

Relation	P no	Pattern specification	Example
Hyponymy	1	X: (w*) (w_{adj}) (w*) Y *punc* (w*). where X is noun, Y is a noun root. (X-Y)	göl: Önceden denizken kurumalar, çekilmeler yüzünden göl durumuna gelmiş yer.**(göl-yer)** *lake: a piece of land, previously existing as sea and becoming dry due to droughts, turns into a small body of water* ***(lake-land)***
	2	X: (w*) (w_{adv}) ($w^*_{no\_punct}$) (Y) *punc* (w*) where X is verb, w_{adv} is a derived adverb, Y is a verb. (X-Y)	hicvetmek: Alay yoluyla yermek.(**hicvetmek-yermek**) *satirize: To criticize by mocking* ***(satirize-criticize)***
	3	X Y : w*. where X and Y is an indefinite noun phrase (X Y-Y)	ada çayı: Bu bitkiden yapılan sıcak içecek.**(ada çayı-çay)** *sage tea: The tea that is made of this plant* ***(sage tea-tea)***
	4	X: w* w_{noun} Y *punc* w*. where w_{noun} and Y compose a noun phrase. (X-Y)	post : Tüylü hayvan derisi. **(post-deri)** *fur : Hairy animal skin.* ***(fur-skin)***
	5	X : w* Y türü*(kind of)* | tipi*(type of)* | çeşidi*(sort of)*. where X and Y nouns (X-Y)	limuzin: İçinde her türlü donanım bulunan lüks, uzun ve geniş otomobil türü.**(limuzin-otomobil)** *limousine: The type of long, wide and luxury automobile in which there exist various equipment* ***(limousine- automobile)***
Synonymy	1	X : w* *punc* Y where X and Y are nouns, adverbs, or adjectives (X-Y)	pinhan: Gizli, saklı, gizlenmiş.**(pinhan-saklı)** *latent: Ulterior, hidden, covert. (latent-hidden)*
	2	Z : w* *punc* X, Y *punc* w* where X, Y have equal chain of suffixes and they are verbs, adjectives or nouns (X-Y)	razı: Uygun bulan, benimseyen, isteyen, kabul eden **(benimsemek-istemek)** *willing : The one who approves, embraces, wants, agrees on sth.* ***(embrace-want)***
Group-of	1	X: w* Y bütünü*(whole of)* | topluluğu*(group of)* | tümü*(all of)* | kümesi*(set of)* | sürüsü*(flock of)* | birliği*(union of)* w* where X and Y are nouns. (X-Y)	âlem: Hayvan veya bitkilerin bütünü.**(alem - bitki)** *kingdom : The whole of plants or animals.* ***(kingdom-plant)***
Antonym	1	X: w* Y olmayan*(not)* | karşıtı*(the opposite of)*. where X and Y are nouns or adjectives. (X-Y)	acı: Bazı maddelerin dilde bıraktığı yakıcı duyu, tatlı karşıtı. **(acı-tatlı)** *bitter: The feeling of pain which some matters leave on tongue, the opposite of sweet.* ***(bitter-sweet)***
Member-of	1	X: w* Y sınıfı*(class of)* | üyesi*(member of)* | takımı*(set of)*. where X and Y are nouns (X-Y)	senatör: Senato üyesi.**(senatör-senato)** *senator: Member of senate.(senator-senate)*
	2	X : Ygillerden*(from the family of Y)* | Ylerden*(from the family of Y)* w*. where X and Y nouns. (X-Y)	çakal: Etoburlardan, sürü hâlinde yaşayan, kurttan küçük bir yaban hayvanı.**(çakal-etobur)** *jackal: From carnivora, a kind of wild animal smaller than wolf, which lives in flocks.* ***(jackal-carnivora)***
Amount-of	1	X: w* Y miktarı*(amount-of)* | ölçüsü*(measure-of)* | birimi*(unit-of)* . where X and Y are nouns (X-Y)	amper: Elektrik akımında şiddet birimi.**(amper-şiddet)** *amper: The unit of intensity in electrical current.* ***(amper- intensity)***
Has-a	1	X: w* Y [w_{noun}] *punc* w*. where Y has the suffix of 'LI', X and Y are nouns (X-Y)	sof : Bir çeşit sertçe, ince yünlü kumaş. **(sof,yün)** *alpaca : A kind of hard, thin, wooled cloth.* ***(alpaca, wool)***

Table 3: The obtained patterns for each type of relation

1. {Icerik:atan Kok:ata tip:FIIL} Ekler:FIIL_KOK+FIIL_EDILGENSESLI_N

   {Content : be assigned Root : assign Pos: Verb} Suffixes : Verb Root + Passive

2. {Icerik:atan Kok:ata tip:ISIM} Ekler:ISIM_KOK+ISIM_SAHIPLIK_SEN_IN

   {Content : your ancestor Root : ancestor Pos: Noun} Suffixes : Noun Root + Possesive_you

3. {Icerik:atan Kok:at tip:FIIL} Ekler:FIIL_KOK+ FIIL_DONUSUM_EN

   {Content : the one throws Root : throw Pos: Verb} Suffixes : Verb Root + Participle

Figure 1: The morphological analysis result of the word atan*(be assigned | your ancestor | the one who throws)*

```
function SIMPLIFIED LESK(word,sentence) returns best sense of word
        best-sense <- most frequent sense for word
        max-overlap <- 0
        context <- set of words in sentence
        for each sense in senses of word do
           signature <- set of words in the gloss and examples of sense
           overlap <- COMPUTEOVERLAP (signature,context)
           if overlap > max-overlap then
              max-overlap <- overlap
              best-sense <- sense
end return (best-sense)
```

Figure 2: Simplified Lesk algorithm

Relation	Pattern	Number of Relations	Accuracy %	Accuracy(ambiguous) %
Hyponymy	1	20566	84	94
	2	1448	84	89
	3	5127	84	90
	4	3502	74	95
	5	387	90	96
Synonymy	1	2313	76	88
	2	22518	96	100
Group-of	1	435	87	97
Antonym	1	380	99	100
Member-of	1	128	92	97
	2	634	100	100
Amount-of	1	119	81	92
Has a	1	2430	82	89
Total		59987	86,85	94,38
NET		58125		

Table 4: The number of relations and the accuracy results for each relation and each pattern rule

It should be considered that the number of relations extracted per pattern is counted individually in order to show the performance of each pattern separately. Some of the relations can be extracted by different patterns of that relation type, so the net total, which is cleaned from the repetitions, is less than overall total.

The results are promising in terms of both the comprehensiveness and the accuracy. If some more effort can be spent on word sense disambiguation, the accuracy may rise to a considerable ratio. The comprehensiveness is intended to be increased with further work, which is discussed in the following section.

The numbers of relation instances are quite greater when compared to BalkaNet project. There are nearly 34,000 relation instances in the project, including the synonym relations among synset members. In this study 58,000 relations are available. Also, it is more likely to be extendible, since not only string patterns but also structural patterns are benefitted from, which will be increased with future work.

4 Conclusion

The semantic relations between the words are extracted in order to develop a semantic network. Some basic relation types such as is-a, group-of, synonym-of, etc. are targeted to obtain an initial network to be extended with further work.

The words are investigated according to their definition in the TLA dictionary. Some row patterns which consist of morphological features of the words, parts of speech or strings in some specific positions and compound words are defined. After that, the dictionary is scanned for searching the definitions that matches one of these patterns. Depending on the results, patterns are reformed and additional features are inserted with the purpose of increasing pattern quality and number of matches. Exact senses of the words are tried to be matched by applying a word sense disambiguation algorithm.

The study has shown that, by taking advantage of the morphological richness of Turkish language and using some structural patterns, it is possible to construct a reasonable semantic network. This study can pave the way for more complex NLP applications and can be used for improving ordinary processes such as word sense disambiguation. The network can be converted into a knowledge base by inserting more accurate relationships and investigating larger and more comprehensive corpora as the future work.

5 Future Work

There is a set of processes to do both for improving and extending the network. Firstly, in order to eliminate erroneous connections from the obtained network, statistical information such as co-occurrence of the words can be investigated. The assumption here is that if two words are related to each other, the possibility of their being together in a corpus increases. The existing connections can be verified or ranked in terms of their reliability by using such information.

In addition, to remove erroneous sense determination, word sense disambiguation method can be improved. After obtaining a reliable, small network, which will serve as seed, new patterns can be extracted by following Turney (2006) and by using these patterns more instances can be extracted from larger corpora. As an alternative, the words can be first tagged with concrete or abstract labels automatically. This information can limit the types of connections a word can contribute. For example, an abstract word cannot connect to another word with a part-whole relation. For this task, a pre-processing step should be applied to classify the words as concrete or abstract.

In addition, with the purpose of improving the network, some other resources will be benefitted from. The existing patterns will be applied to Wikipedia (http://www.wikipedia.org/) entries, by selecting only the definitions of the concepts. An advantage of this process is that it can be re-performed periodically to keep the network up-to-date and dynamic. Also, the number of relation types will be increased. Currently, only the nouns, noun phrases consisting from two words, adjectives and verbs are handled. Also, only the relationships within the same type of words are extracted that is, a noun can be connected only to another noun, not an adjective or a verb. Finer grained relationships can establish connections among different parts of speech.

References

Barrière Caroline. 1997. From a children's first dictionary to a lexical knowledge base of conceptual graphs. PhD thesis. Simon Fraser University, Canada.

Bilgin Orhan, Çetinoğlu Özlem, and Oflazer Kemal. 2004. Morphosemantic Relations In and Across Wordnets: A Preliminary Study Based on Turkish. Proceedings of the Global WordNet Conference. Masaryk, Czech Republic.

http://people.sabanciuniv.edu/~oflazer/balkanet/twn_tr.htm

Celli Fabio, Nissim Malvina. 2009. Automatic identification of semantic relations in Italian complex nominals. Proceedings of the 8th International Conference on Computational Semantics, Tilburg. pp. 45-60.

Fellbaum, Christiane. 1998. WordNet: An Electronic Lexical Database. Cambridge, MA: MIT Press.

Havasi Catherina, Speer Robert, and Alonso B. Jason. 2007. ConceptNet 3: a Flexible, Multilingual Semantic Network for Common Sense Knowledge. Proceedings of the 22nd Conference on Artificial Intelligence.

Lesk, E. Micheal. 1986. Automatic sense disambiguation using machine readable dictionaries: how to tell a pine cone from an ice cream cone. In SIGDOC '86: Proceedings of the 5th annual international conference on Systems documentation, pages 24-26, New York, NY, USA. ACM.

Miller, George A. 1995. WordNet: A Lexical Database for English. Communications of the ACM Vol. 38, No. 11: 39-41.

Nakov Preslav, Hearts A. Marti. 2008. Solving Relational Similarity Problems Using the Web as a Corpus, Proceedings of ACL-08: HLT, Columbus, Ohio, USA. pp. 452–460.

Pantel Patrick, Pennacchiotti Marco. 2006. Espresso: Leveraging Generic Patterns for Automatically Harvesting Semantic Relations, Proceedings of the 21st International Conference on Computational Linguistics and 44th Annual Meeting of the ACL. Sydney, Australia. pp. 113-120.

Turney D. Peter. 2006. Expressing implicit semantic relations without supervision. Proceedings of the 21st International Conference on Computational Linguistics and 44th Annual Meeting of the ACL. Sydney, Australia. pp. 313-320.

Önder Pınar. 2009. Design and Implementation of the semantic Turkish Language and Dialects Dictionary. MS thesis. Fatih University, İstanbul.

Identifying Event – Sentiment Association using Lexical Equivalence and Co-reference Approaches

Anup Kumar Kolya[1] **Dipankar Das**[1] **Asif Ekbal**[2] **Sivaji Bandyopadhyay**[1]
[1] Computer Science and Engineering Department, Jadavpur University, India
[2] Indian Institute of Technology, Patna (IITP), India
anup.kolya@gmail.com, dipankar.dipnil2005@gmail.com
asif.ekbal@gmail.com, sivaji_cse_ju@yahoo.com

Abstract

In this paper, we have identified event and sentiment expressions at word level from the sentences of TempEval-2010 corpus and evaluated their association in terms of lexical equivalence and co-reference. A hybrid approach that consists of Conditional Random Field (CRF) based machine learning framework in conjunction with several rule based strategies has been adopted for event identification within the TimeML framework. The strategies are based on semantic role labeling, WordNet relations and some handcrafted rules. The sentiment expressions are identified simply based on the cues that are available in the sentiment lexicons such as *Subjectivity Wordlist*, *SentiWordNet* and *WordNet Affect*. The identification of lexical equivalence between event and sentiment expressions based on the part-of-speech (POS) categories is straightforward. The emotional verbs from *VerbNet* have also been employed to improve the coverage of lexical equivalence. On the other hand, the association of sentiment and event has been analyzed using the notion of co-reference. The parsed dependency relations along with basic rhetoric knowledge help to identify the co-reference between event and sentiment expressions. Manual evaluation on the 171 sentences of TempEval-2010 dataset yields the *precision*, *recall* and *F-Score* values of 61.25%, 70.29% and 65.23% respectively.

1 Introduction

Event and Sentiment are two abstract entities closely coupled with each other from social, psychological and commercial perspectives. Some kind of action that is going on or something that is being happened are addressed as *events* in general by the Natural Language (NL) researchers. The events are described in texts where the time, temporal location and ordering of the events are specified. Event entities are represented by finite clauses, nonfinite clauses, nominalizations, event-referring nouns, adjectives and even some kinds of adverbial clauses.

On the other hand, text not only contains the informative contents, but also some attitudinal private information that includes sentiments. Nowadays, in the NLP communities, research activities on sentiment analysis are in full swing. But, the identification of sentiment from texts is not an easy task as it is not open to any objective observation or verification (Quirk *et al.*, 1985).

Sometimes, similar or different types of sentiments are expressed on a single or multiple events. Sentiment of people over different events is important as it has great influence on our society. Tracking users' sentiments about products or events or about political candidates as expressed in online forums, customer relationship management, stock market prediction, social networking etc., temporal question answering, document summarization, information retrieval systems are some of the important applications of sentiment analysis.

The identification of the association between event and sentiment is becoming more popular and interesting research challenge in the area of Natural Language Processing (NLP). Our present task is to identify the event and sentiment expressions from the text, analyze their associative relationship and investigate the insides of event-sentiment relations.

For example, in the following sentence, the annotated events are, ***talked***, ***sent*** and ***hijacked*** .But, it also shows the presence of underlying *sentiments* (as shown in underlined script) inscribed in the sentence. Here, sentiment helps to evoke the event property at lexical entity level (e.g. negative (-ve) sentiment for only the event word *hijacked*) as well as at context level (e.g. positive (+ve) sentiment associated with the event *hijacked* as the event word appears with the evaluative expression, *recover* that gives the +ve polarity).

"The prime minister of India told Friday that he has ***talked*** with top commander of Indian military force and ***sent*** a team to *recover the host of Taj Hotel* ***hijacked***."

Hence, we have organized the entire task into three different steps i) event identification, ii) sentiment expression identification and iii) identification of event sentiment relationships at context level using lexical equivalence and co-reference approaches.

In the first step, we propose a hybrid approach for event extraction from the text under the TempEval-2010 framework. Initially, we have used a Conditional Random Field (CRF) (Lafferty *et al.*, 2001) machine learning framework but we observe that it often makes the errors in extracting the events denoted by *deverbial* entities. This observation prompts us to employ several strategies in conjunction with machine learning. These strategies are implemented based on semantic role labeling, WordNet (Miller, 1990) and some handcrafted rules. We have experimented with the TempEval-2010 evaluation challenge setup (Kolya *et al.*, 2010). Evaluation results yield the *precision*, *recall* and *F-measure* values of approximately 93.00%, 96.00% and 94.47% respectively. This is approximately 12% higher *F-measure* in comparison to the best system (Llorens *et al.*, 2010) of TempEval-2010.

On the other hand, the identification of the sentiment expressions is carried out based on the sentiment word. The words are searched in three different sentiment lexicons, the *Subjectivity Word lists* (Banea *et al.*, 2008), *SentiWordNet* (Baccianella *et al.*, 2010) and *WordNet Affect* (Strapparava and Valitutti, 2004). The coarse-grained (*positive* and *negative*) as well as Ekman's (1993) six fine-grained sentiment or emotion expressions (*happy, sadness, anger, disgust, fear* and *surprise*) are tagged in the corpus. As there is no annotation in the TemEval-2010 corpus for sentiment expressions, the evaluation has been carried out by the authors and it achieves the *precision*, *recall* and *F-measure* values of approximately 73.54%, 86.04% and 79.30% respectively

Determining the lexical equivalence of event and sentiment expressions based on the POS property at the lexical entity level is straightforward. If an event word also expresses the sentiment word, we have associated the corresponding sentiment type with the event word directly. In addition to the sentiment lexicons, the emotional verbs extracted from the *VerbNet* (Kipper-Schuler, 2005) are used in this phase. It improves the coverage of lexical equivalence by 12.76%.

But, if the event and sentiment expressions occupy separate text spans in a sentence, we have adopted a co-reference approach for identifying their association. The parsed dependency relations along with some basic rhetoric components, such as *nucleus, satellite* and *locus* help in identifying the co-reference between the event and sentiment expressions. The text span containing sentiment word is hypothesized as the *locus*, the main effective part of the *nucleus* or *satellite*. The text span that reflects the primary goal of the writer is termed as *nucleus* (marked as "{ }") whereas the span that provides supplementary material is termed as *satellite* (marked as "[ ]"). The distinguished identification of *nucleus* and *satellite* as well as their separation from each other is carried out based on the *direct* and *transitive* dependency relations, *causal verbs*, *relaters* or *discourse markers*. If both the *locus* and event are identified together in either *nucleus* or *satellite*, we term their association as co-referenced. If they occur separately in *nucleus* and *satellite* and share at least one *direct* dependency relation, we consider their association as co-referenced.

The evaluation of the lexical equivalence as well as co-reference systems has been performed by the authors. Primarily, the evaluation of both systems has been conducted on the random samples of 200 sentences of the TempEval-2010 training dataset. Finally, the co-reference system achieves the *precision*, *recall* and *F-Scores* of

61.25%, 70.29% and 65.23% respectively on 171 sentences of the TempEval-2010 test corpus.

The rest of the paper is organized as follows. Section 2 describes the related work. The event identification is discussed in Section 3. The identification of sentiment expressions is described in Section 4. Determination of lexical equivalence between event and sentiment expressions is specified in Section 5. The co-reference approach for identifying the association between event and sentiment is described in Section 6. Finally Section 7 concludes the paper.

2 Related Work

The existing works on event extraction are based either on pattern-matching rules (Mani and Wilson 2000), or on the machine learning approach (Boguraev and Ando, 2005). But, still the problems persist with the high complexities involved in the proper extractions of events. The events expressions were annotated in the TempEval 2007 source in accordance with the TimeML standard (Pustejovsky *et al.*, 2003). On the other hand, the Task B of TempEval-2010 evaluation challenge setup (Verhagen *et al.*, 2010) was aimed at identifying events from text. The best achieved result was obtained by (Llorens *et al.*, 2010).

The majority of subjective analysis methods that are related to emotion is based on textual keywords spotting that use specific lexical resources. A lexicon that provides appraisal attributes for terms was constructed and the features were used for emotion classification (Whitelaw *et al.*, 2005). The features along with the bag-of-words model give 90.2% accuracy. UPAR7 (Chaumartin, 2007), a rule-based system uses a combination of *WordNet Affect* and *SentiWordNet.* The system was semi-automatically enriched with the original trial data provided during the SemEval task (Strapparava and Mihalcea, 2007). SWAT (Katz *et al.*, 2007) is another supervised system that uses a unigram model trained to annotate emotional content.

Our motivation is that though events and sentiments are closely coupled with each other from social, psychological and commercial perspectives, very little attention has been given about their detection and analysis. To the best of our knowledge, only a few tasks have been attempted (Fukuhara *et al.*, 2007) (Das *et al.*, 2010).

Sometimes, the opinion topics are not necessarily spatially coherent as there may be two opinions in the same sentence on different topics, as well as opinions that are on the same topic separated by opinions that do not share that topic (Stoyanov and Cardie 2008). The authors have established their hypothesis by applying the co-reference technique. Similarly, we have adopted the co-reference technique based on basic rhetoric components for identifying the association between event and sentiment expressions. In addition to that, we have also employed the lexical equivalence approach for identifying their association.

3 Event Identification

In this work, we propose a hybrid approach for event identification from the text under the TempEval-2010 framework. We use Conditional Random Field (CRF) as the underlying machine learning algorithm. We observe that this machine learning based system often makes the errors in identifying the events denoted by *deverbial* entities. This observation prompts us to employ several strategies in conjunction with machine learning techniques. These strategies have been implemented based on semantic role labeling, WordNet senses and some handcrafted rules.

We have experiment with the TempEval-2010 evaluation challenge setup (Kolya *et al.*, 2010). Evaluation results yield the precision, recall and F-measure values of approximately 93.00%, 96.00% and 94.47% respectively. This is approximately 12% higher F-measure in comparison to the best system (Llorens *et al.*, 2010) of TempEval-2010.

3.1 CRF based Approach for Event Identification

We extract the gold-standard TimeBank features for events in order to train/test the CRF model. In the present work, we mainly use the various combinations of the following features:

Part of Speech (POS) of event terms (e.g. Adjective, Noun and Verb), **Tense** (Present, Past, Future, Infinitive, Present part, Past part, or NONE), **Aspect** (Progressive, Perfective and Perfective Progressive or NONE), **Class** (*Reporting, Perception, Aspectual, I_action, I_state, State, Occurrence*), **Stem** (e.g., discount /s/).

3.2 Use of Semantic Roles for Event Identification

We use an open source Semantic Role Labeler [1](SRL) (Gildea *et al.*, 2002) (Pradhan *et al.*, 2004) to identify different features of the sentences. For each predicate in a sentence acting as event word, semantic roles extract all constituents, determining their arguments (agent, patient etc.) and adjuncts (locative, temporal etc.). Semantic roles can be used to detect the events that are the nominalizations of verbs such as *agreement* for *agree* or *construction* for *construct*. Nominalizations (or, *deverbal nouns*) are commonly defined as nouns that are morphologically derived from verbs, usually by suffixation (Quirk *et al.*, 1985). Event nominalizations often afford the same semantic roles as verbs and often replace them in written language (Gurevich *et al.*, 2006). Event nominalizations constitute the bulk of *deverbal* nouns. The following example sentence shows how semantic roles can be used for event identification.

[$_{ARG1}$ ***All sites****]* were *[$_{TARGET}$* ***inspected****]* to the satisfaction of the inspection team and with full cooperation of Iraqi authorities, *[$_{ARG0}$* ***Dacey****]* *[$_{TARGET}$* ***said****]*.

The extracted target words are treated as the event words. It has been observed that many of these target words are identified as the event expressions by the CRF model. But, there exists many nominalised event expressions (i.e., *deverbal nouns*) that are not identified as events by the supervised CRF. These nominalised expressions are correctly identified as events by SRL.

3.3 Use of WordNet for Event Identification

WordNet is mainly used to identify *non-deverbal event nouns*. We observed that the event entities like '*war*', '*attempt*', '*tour*' are not properly identified. These words have noun (NN) POS information as the previous approaches, i.e., CRF and SRL can only identify those event words that have verb (VB) POS information. We know from the lexical information of WordNet that the words like '*war*' and '*tour*' are generally used as both *noun* and *verb* forms in the sentence. Therefore, we have designed the following two rules based on the WordNet:

Rule 1: The word tokens having Noun (NN) POS categories are looked into the WordNet. If it appears in the WordNet with noun and verb senses, then that word token is considered as an event. For example, *war* has both noun and verb senses in the WordNet, and hence *war* is considered as an event.

Rule 2: The *stems* of the noun word tokens are looked into the WordNet. If one of the WordNet senses is verb then the token is considered as verb. For example, the stem of *proposal*, i.e., *propose* has two different senses, noun and verb in the WordNet, and thus it is considered as an event.

3.4 Use of Rules for Event Identification

Here, we mainly concentrate on the identification of specific lexical classes like '*inspection*' and '*resignation*'. These can be identified by the suffixes such as ('*-ción*'), ('*-tion*') or ('*-ion*'), i.e., the morphological markers of *deverbal* derivations.

Initially, we have employed the CRF based Stanford Named Entity (NE) tagger[2] on the TempEval-2 test dataset. The output of the system is tagged with *Person*, *Location*, *Organization* and *Other* classes. The words starting with the capital letters are also considered as NEs. Thereafter, we came up with the following rules for event identification:

Cue-1: The *deverbal* nouns are usually identified by the suffixes like '*-tion*', '*-ion*', '*-ing*' and '*-ed*' etc. The nouns that are not NEs, but end with these suffixes are considered as the event words.

Cue 2: The verb-noun combinations are searched in the sentences of the test set. The non-NE noun word tokens are considered as the events.

Cue 3: Nominals and non-*deverbal* event nouns can be identified by the complements of aspectual PPs headed by prepositions like *during*, *after* and *before*, and complex prepositions such as *at the end of* and *at the beginning of* etc. The next word token(s) appearing after these clue word(s) or phrase(s) are considered as events.

[1] http://cemantix.org/assert.html

[2] http://nlp.stanford.edu/software/CRF-NER.shtml

Cue 4: The non-NE nouns occurring after the expressions such as *frequency of*, *occurrence of* and *period of* are most probably the event nouns.

Cue 5: Event nouns can also appear as objects of aspectual and time-related verbs, such as *have begun a campaign* or *have carried out a campaign* etc. The non-NEs that appear after the expressions like "*have begun a*", "*have carried out a*" etc. are also denoted as the events.

4 Sentiment Expression Identification

Sentiment is an important cue that effectively describes the events associated with it. The binary classification of the sentiments (*positive* and *negative*) as well as the fine-grained categorization into Ekman's (1993) six emotions is therefore employed for identifying the sentiment expressions. 200 sentences are randomly selected from the training dataset of the TempEval-2010 corpus. These sentences have been considered as our development set. On the other hand, 171 sentences were already provided as the test sentences in the TempEval-2010 evaluation challenge.

The events are already annotated in the TempEval-2010 corpus. But, no sentiment or emotion related annotation is available in the corpus. Hence, we have annotated the sentiment expressions at word level in a semi-supervised way. The word level entities are tagged by their coarse and fine grained sentiment tags using the available sentiment related lexical resources. Then the automatic annotation has been evaluated manually by the authors. The semi-supervised sentiment annotation agreements were 90.23% for the development set and 92.45% for the test sets respectively.

4.1 Lexicon based Approach

The tagging of the *evaluative expressions* or more specifically the sentiment expressions on the TempEval-2010 corpus has been carried out using the available sentiment lexicons. We passed the sentences through three sentiment lexicons, *Subjectivity Wordlists* (Banea *et al.*, 2008), *SentiWordNet* (Baccianella *et al.*, 2010) and *WordNet Affect* (Strapparava and Valitutti, 2004). *Subjectivity Wordlist* assigns words with the strong or weak subjectivity and prior polarities of types *positive*, *negative* and *neutral*. *SentiWordNet*, used in opinion mining and sentiment analysis, assigns three sentiment scores such as *positive*, *negative* and *objective* to each synset of *WordNet*. *WordNet Affect*, a small well-used lexical resource but valuable for its affective annotation contains the words that convey emotion.

The algorithm is that, if a word in a sentence is present in any of these resources; the word is tagged as the sentiment expression. But, if any word is not found in any of them, each word of the sentence is passed through the WordNet Morphological analyzer (Miller, 1990) to identify its root form and the root form is searched through the resources again. If the root form is found, the corresponding word is tagged as sentiment expression accordingly.

The identified sentiment expressions have been evaluated by the authors and it achieves the *precision, recall* and *F-Score* of 73.54%, 86.04% and 79.30%, respectively on a total of 171 test sentences of the TempEval-2010 corpus.

The identification of event words that also express sentiment is straightforward. But, the problem arises when the event and sentiment expressions are present separately in a sentence and the sentiment is either closely associated with the event or affects it. In case of the former, we have adopted the approach of lexical equivalence between the event and sentiment entities whereas the co-reference technique has been introduced for resolving the latter case.

5 Lexical Equivalence between Event and Sentiment Expressions

It is observed that in general the verbs, nouns and adjectives represent events. The sentences are passed through an open source Stanford Maximum Entropy based POS tagger (Manning and Toutanova, 2000). The best reported accuracy for the POS tagger on the Penn Treebank is 96.86% overall and 86.91% on previously unseen words. Our objective was to identify the event words that also express sentiments. Hence, we have identified the event words that have also been tagged as the sentiment expressions. The coverage of these lexical resources in identifying the event sentiment association is shown in Table 1.

On the other hand, not only the adjectives or nouns, the sentiment or emotional verbs play an important role in identifying the sentiment expressions. Hence, in addition to the above mentioned sentiment resources, we have also incorporated English *VerbNet* (Kipper-Schuler, 2005) for the automatic annotation process. *VerbNet* associates the semantics of a verb with its syntactic frames and combines traditional lexical semantic information such as thematic roles and semantic predicates, with syntactic frames and selectional restrictions. Verb entries in the same *VerbNet* class share common syntactic frames and thus they are believed to have the same syntactic behavior. For example, the emotional verbs "*love*" and "*enjoy*" are members of the *admire-31.2-1* class and "*enjoy*" also belongs to the class *want-32.1-1*.

The XML files of *VerbNet* are preprocessed to build up a general list that contains all member verbs and their available syntax information retrieved from VerbNet. The main criterion for selecting the member verbs as sentiment expressions is the presence of "*emotional_state*" type predicate in their frame semantics. The frequencies of the event words matched against the above said four resources are shown in Table 1. It has been observed that the adjective events are not identified by the lexical resources as their frequency in the test corpus was very low. But, the lexical coverage has been improved by 12.76% by incorporating *VerbNet*.

Resources	Noun #114	Adjective #4	Verb #380
Subjectivity Wordlists	24	--	35
SentiWordNet	32	--	59
WordNet Affect List	12	--	25
VerbNet (emotional verbs)	--	--	**79**
Accuracy (in %)	59.64		52.57

Table 1: Results of Lexical Equivalence between Event and Sentiment based on different resources

6 Co-reference between Event and Sentiment Expressions

The opinion and/or sentiment topics are not necessarily spatially coherent as there may be two opinions in the same sentence on different topics. Sometimes, the opinions that are on the same topic are separated by opinions that do not share that topic (Stoyanov and Cardie, 2008). We observe the similar situation in case of associating sentiments with events. Hence, the hypothesis for opinion topic is established for sentiment events by applying the co-reference technique along with the rhetorical structure. We have proposed two different systems for identifying the association of sentiments with the events at context level.

6.1 Baseline Co-reference System

The baseline system has been developed based on the *object* information present in the dependency relations of the parsed sentences. Stanford Parser (Marneffe *et al.*, 2006), a probabilistic lexicalized parser containing 45 different part of speech (POS) tags of Pen Treebank tagset has been used to get the parsed sentences and dependency relations. The dependency relations are checked for the predicates "*dobj*" so that the related components present in the predicate are considered as the probable candidates for the events.

If a dependency relation contains both the event and sentiment words, we have considered the presence of co-reference between them. But, it has been observed that the event and sentiment expressions are also present in two different relations that share a common word element. Hence, if the event and sentiment words appear in two different relations but both of the relations contain at least one common element, the event and sentiment words are termed as co-referenced.

Overall, the baseline co-reference system achieves the *precision*, *recall* and *F-Scores* of 40.03%, 46.10% and 42.33% for event-sentiment co-reference identification. For example in the following sentence, the writer's direct as well as indirect emotional intentions are reflected by mentioning one or more topics or events (*spent*, *thought*) and their associated sentiments (*great*).

"When Wong Kwan ***spent*** seventy million dollars for this house, he ***thought*** it was a ***great*** deal."

The baseline co-reference system fails to associate the sentiment expressions with their corresponding event expressions. Hence, we aimed for the rhetoric structure based co-reference system to identify their association.

6.2 Rhetoric Co-reference System

The distribution of events and sentiment expressions in different text spans of a sentence needs the analysis of sentential structure. We have incorporated the knowledge of Rhetorical Structure Theory (RST) (Mann and Thompson 1987) for identifying the events that are co-referred by their corresponding sentiment expressions.

The theory maintains that consecutive discourse elements, termed *text spans*, are related by a relatively small set (20–25) of *rhetorical relations*. But, instead of identifying the rhetorical relations, the present task acquires the basic and coarse rhetorical components such as *locus*, *nucleus* and *satellite* from a sentence. These rhetoric clues help in identifying the individual event span associated with the span denoting the corresponding sentiment expression in a sentence. The text span that reflects the primary goal of the writer is termed as *nucleus* (marked as "{ }") whereas the span that provides supplementary material is termed as *satellite* (marked as "[ ]"). For example, the *nucleus* and *satellite* textual spans are shown in the following sentence as,

{Traders said the market remains extremely nervous} because [the wild swings seen on the New York Stock Exchange last week].

The event or topic of an opinion or sentiment depends on the context in which the associated opinion or sentiment expression occurs (Stoyanov and Cardie 2008). Considering the similar hypothesis in case of events instead of topics, the co-reference between an event and a sentiment expression is identified from the *nucleus* and/or *satellite* by positioning the sentiment expression as *locus*. We have also incorporated the WordNet's (Miller 1990) morphological analyzer to identify the stemmed forms of the sentiment words.

The preliminary separation of *nucleus* from *satellite* was carried out based on the list of frequently used *causal keywords* (e.g., *as, because, that, while, whether etc*) and punctuation markers (,) (!) (?).The *discourse markers* and *causal verbs* are also the useful clues if they are explicitly specified in the text. The identification of *discourse markers* from written text itself is a research area (Azar 1999). Hence, our task was restricted to identify only the explicit *discourse markers* that are tagged by *conjunctive_*() or *mark_*() type dependency relations of the parsed constituents. The dependency relations containing *conjunctive* markers (e.g., *conj_and*(), *conj_or*(), *conj_but*()) were considered for separating *nucleus* from *satellite* if the markers are present in between two successive clauses. Otherwise, the word token contained in the *mark_*() type dependency relation was considered as a *discourse marker*.

The list of *causal* verbs is prepared by processing the XML files of *VerbNet*. If any *VerbNet* class file contains any frame with semantic type as *Cause,* we collect the member verbs of that XML class file and term the member verbs as *causal verbs*. We used a list that contains a total number of 253 *causal verbs*.

If any clause tagged as *S* or *SBAR* in the parse tree contains any *causal verb*, that clause is considered as the *nucleus* and the rest of the clauses denote the *satellites*. Considering the basic theory of rhetorical structure (Mann and Thompson 1987), the clauses were separated into *nucleus* and *satellite* to identify the event and sentiment expressions.

The *direct* dependency is identified based on the simultaneous presence of *locus* and the *event* word in the same dependency relation whereas the *transitive* dependency is verified if the word is connected to *locus* and *event* via one or more intermediate dependency relations.

If the event and sentiment words are together present in either *nucleus* or *satellite*, the association between the two expressions is considered as co-referenced. If they occur in *nucleus* and *satellite* separately, but the event and sentiment words are present in at least one *direct* dependency relation, the expressions are termed as co-referenced.

In the previous example, the event expressions, "*said*" and "*remains*" are associated with the sentiment expression "*nervous*" as both the event expressions share the *direct* dependency relations "*cop(nervous-7, remains-5)*" and "*ccomp(said-2, nervous-7)*" in the *nucleus* segment. Similarly, the event word, "*seen*" and sentiment word "*wild*" are present in the *satellite* part and they share a *direct* dependency relation "*partmod(swings-12, seen-13)*". But, no *direct* dependency relation is present between the "*nervous*" and "*seen*" or "*said*" and "*wild*" or "*remains*" and "*wild*".

6.3 Results

Though the event annotation is specified in the TempEval-2010 corpus, the association between the event and sentiment expressions was not specified in the corpus. Hence, we have carried out the evaluation manually. The 200 random samples of the training set that were used in sentiment expression identification task have been considered as our development set. The Evaluation Vectors (*EvalV*) are prepared manually from each sentence of the development and test sets. The vectors <*EvExp, SentiExp*> are filled with the annotated events and sentiment expressions by considering their association. The annotation of sentiment expressions using the semi-supervised process has been described in Section 4.

The rule based baseline and rhetoric based co-reference systems identify the event and sentiment expressions from each sentence and stores them in a Co-reference Vector (*CorefV*). The evaluation is carried out by comparing the system generated Co-reference Vectors (*CorefV*) with their corresponding Evaluation Vectors (*EvalV*). The evaluation results on 171 test sentences are shown in Table 2.

Co-reference Approaches	Prec. (in %)	Rec.	F-Score
Baseline System	40.03	46.10	42.33
Rhetoric System	61.25	70.29	65.23

Table 2: *Precision* (Prec.), *Recall* (Rec.) and *F-Scores* (in %) of the event-sentiment co-reference systems

Overall, the *precision*, *recall* and *F-Scores* are 61.25%, 70.29% and 65.23% for event-sentiment co-reference identification using rhetoric clues. Though the co-reference technique performs satisfactorily for identifying the event-sentiment co-reference, the problem arises in distinguishing the corresponding spans of events from an overlapped text span of multi-word tokens.

7 Conclusion

In this present work, we have identified event and sentiment expressions at word level from the sentences of TempEval-2010 corpus and evaluated their association in terms of lexical equivalence and co-reference. It has been observed that the lexical equivalence based on lexicons performs satisfactorily but overall, the co-reference entails that the presence of indirect affective clues can also be traced with the help of rhetoric knowledge and dependency relations. The association of the sentiments with their corresponding events can be used in future concerning the time based sentiment change over events.

Acknowledgments

The work is supported by a grant from the India-Japan Cooperative Programme (DST-JST) 2009 Research project entitled "Sentiment Analysis where AI meets Psychology" funded by Department of Science and Technology (DST), Government of India.

References

Baccianella Stefano, Esuli Andrea and Sebas-tiani Fabrizio. 2010. SentiWordNet 3.0: An Enhanced Lexical Re-source for Sentiment Analysis and Opinion Mining. *In Proceedings of the 7th Conference on Language Resources and Evaluation*, pp. 2200-2204.

Banea, Carmen, Mihalcea Rada, Wiebe Janyce. 2008. A Bootstrapping Method for Building Subjectivity Lexicons for Languages with Scarce Resources. *The Sixth International Conference on Language Resources and Evaluation.*

Boguraev, B., Ando, R. K. 2005. *TimeBank-DrivenTimeML Analysis. Annotating, Extracting and Reasoning about Time and Events* 2005.

Chaumartin, F. 2007. Upar7: A knowledge-based system for headline sentiment tagging. *SemEval-200*, Czech Republic.

Ekman Paul. 1993. An argument for basic emotions, *Cognition and Emotion*, 6(3-4):169-200.

Fukuhara T., Nakagawa, H. and Nishida, T. 2007. Understanding Sentiment of People from News Articles: Temporal Sentiment Analysis of Social Events. *ICWSM'2007*, Boulder, Colorado.

Gildea, D. and Jurafsky, D. 2002. Automatic Labeling of Semantic Roles. *Computational Linguistics*, 28(3):245–288.

Gurevich, O., R. Crouch, T. King, and V. de Paiva. 2006. Deverbal Nouns in Knowledge Representation. *Proceedings of FLAIRS*, pages 670–675, Melbourne Beach, FL.

Katz, P., Singleton, M. and Wicentowski, R. 2007. Swat-mp: the semeval-2007 systems for task 5 and task *SemEval-2007.*

Kipper-Schuler, K. 2005. *VerbNet: A broad-coverage, comprehensive verb lexicon.* Ph.D. thesis, Computer and Information Science Dept., University of Pennsylvania, Philadelphia, PA.

Kolya, A., Ekbal, A. and Bandyopadhyay, S. 2010. JU_CSE_TEMP: A First Step towards Evaluating Events, Time Expressions and Temporal Relations. In *Proceedings of the 5th International Workshop on Semantic Evaluation*, ACL 2010, July 15-16, Sweden, pp. 345–350.

Lafferty, J., McCallum, A.K., Pereira, F. 2001. Conditional Random Fields: Probabilistic Models for Segmenting and Labeling Sequence Data. *International Conference on Machine Learning.*

Llorens Hector, Estela Saquete, Borja Navarro. 2010. TIPSem (English and Spanish): Evaluating CRFs and Semantic Roles. *Proceedings of the 5th International Workshop on Semantic Evaluation, ACL 2010*, pages 284–291, Uppsala, Sweden, 15-16 July 2010.

Mani, I., and Wilson G. 2000. Processing of News. *In Proceedings of the 38th Annual Meeting of the Association for Computational Linguistics*, pp. 69-76.

Mann, W. and S. Thompson. 1987. Rhetorical Structure Theory: Description and Construction of Text Structure. In *G. Kempen (ed.), Natural Language Generation*, Martinus Nijhoff, The Hague, pp. 85–96.

Manning Christopher and Toutanova, Kristina. 2000. Enriching the Knowledge Sources Used in a Maximum Entropy Part-of-Speech Tagger. *Proceedings of the Joint SIGDAT Conference on Empirical Methods in Natural Language Processing and Very Large Corpora (EMNLP/VLC)*

Marneffe, Marie-Catherine de, Bill MacCartney, and Christopher D.Manning. 2006. Generating Typed Dependency Parses from Phrase Structure Parses. *5th International Conference on Language Resources and Evaluation.*

Miller George A. 1990. WordNet: An on-line lexical database. *International Journal of Lexicography*, 3(4): 235–312

Pradhan S., Wayne W., Hacioglu, K., Martin, J.H. and Jurafsky, D. 2004. Shallow Semantic Parsing using Support Vector Machines. *Proceedings of the Human Language Technology Conference/North American chapter of the Association for Computational Linguistics annual meeting* Boston, MA, May 2-7.

Pustejovsky, J., Castano, J., Ingria, R., Sauri, R., Gaizauskas, R., Setzer, A., Katz, G. and Radev, D. TimeML: Robust specification of event and temporal expressions in text. *In AAAI Spring Symposium on New Directions in Question-Answering*, pp. 28-34, CA, 2003.

Quirk, R., Greenbaum, S. Leech, G. and Svartvik, J. 1985. A Comprehensive Grammar of the English Language. *Longman.*

Strapparava C. and Valitutti, A. 2004. Wordnet-affect: an affective extension of wordnet. *In 4th International Conference on Language Resources and Evaluation*, pp. 1083-1086.

Strapparava Carlo and Mihalcea Rada. 2007. SemEval-2007 Task 14: Affective Text. *45th Aunual Meeting of Association for Computational linguistics.*

Stoyanov, V., and Cardie, C. 2008. Annotating topics of opinions. In *Proceedings of LREC.*

VigNet: Grounding Language in Graphics using Frame Semantics

Bob Coyne and **Daniel Bauer** and **Owen Rambow**
Columbia University
New York, NY 10027, USA
{coyne, bauer, rambow}@cs.columbia.edu

Abstract

This paper introduces *Vignette Semantics*, a lexical semantic theory based on Frame Semantics that represents conceptual and graphical relations. We also describe a lexical resource that implements this theory, VigNet, and its application in text-to-scene generation.

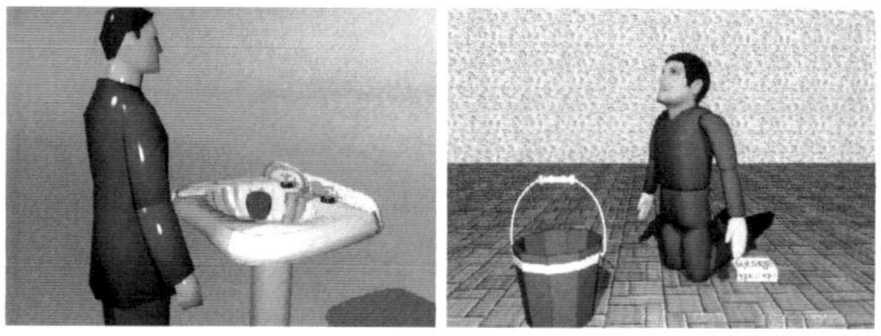

Figure 1: Mocked-up scenes using the WASH-SMALL-FRUIT vignette ("John washes the apple") and WASH-FLOOR-W-SPONGE vignette ("John washes the floor").

1 Introduction

Our goal is to build a comprehensive text-to-graphics system. When considering sentences such as *John is washing an apple* and *John is washing the floor*, we discover that rather different graphical knowledge is needed to generate static scenes representing the meaning of these two sentences (see Figure 1): the human actor is assuming different poses, he is interacting differently with the thing being washed, and the water, present in both scenes, is supplied differently. If we consider the types of knowledge needed for scene generation, we find that we cannot simply associate a single set of knowledge with the English verb *wash*. The question arises: how can we organize this knowledge and associate it with lexical items, so that the resulting lexical knowledge base both is usable in a wide-coverage text-to-graphics system, and can be populated with the required knowledge using limited resources?

In this paper, we present a new knowledge base that we use for text-to-graphics generation. We distinguish three types of knowledge needed for our task. The first is **conceptual knowledge**, which is knowledge about concepts, often evoked by words. For example, if I am told John bought an apple, then I know that that event necessarily also involved the seller and money. Second, we need **world knowledge**. For example, apples grow on trees in certain geographic locations at certain times of the year. Third, we need **grounding knowledge**, which tells us how concepts are related to sensory experiences. In our application, we model grounding knowledge with a database of 3-dimensional graphical models. We will refer to this type of grounding knowledge as **graphical knowledge**. An example of grounding knowledge is knowing that several specific graphical models represent apple trees.

Conceptual knowledge is already the object of extensive work in frame semantics; FrameNet (Ruppenhofer et al., 2010) is an extensive (but not complete) relational semantic encoding of lexical meaning in a frame-semantic conceptual framework. We use this prior work, both the theory and the resource, in our work. The encoding of world knowledge has been the topic of much work in Artificial Intelligence. Our specific contribution in this paper is the integration of the representation for world knowledge and graphical knowledge into a frame-semantic approach. In order to integrate these knowledge types, we extend FrameNet in three manners.

1. Frames describe complex relations between their frame elements, but these relations, i.e.

the internal structure of a frame, is not explicitly formulated in frame semantics. FrameNet frames do not have any intensional meaning besides the informal English definition of the frames (and what is expressed by so-called "frame-to-frame relations"). From the point of view of graphics generation, internal structure is necessary. While for many applications a semantic representation can remain vague, a scene must contain concrete objects and spatial relations between them.

2. Some frames are not semantically specific enough. For example, there is a frame SELF_MOTION, which includes both *walk* and *swim*; these verbs clearly need different graphical realizations, but they are also different from a general semantic point of view. While this situation could be remedied by extending the inventory of frames by adding WALK and SWIM frames, which would inherit from SELF_MOTION, the situation is more complex. Consider *wash an apple* and *wash the floor*, discussed above. While the core meaning of *wash* is the same in both phrases, the graphical realization is again very different. However, we cannot simply create two new frames, since at some level (though not the graphical level) the meaning is indeed compositional. We thus need a new mechanism.

3. FrameNet is a lexical resource that illustrates how language can be used to refer to frames, which are abstract definitions of concepts, and their frame elements. It is not intended to be a formalism for deep semantic interpretation. The FrameNet annotations show the frame elements of frames (e.g. the goal frame element of the SELF_MOTION frame) being filled with text passages (e.g. *into the garden*) rather than with concrete semantic objects (e.g. an 'instance' of a LOCALE_BY_USE frame evoked by *garden*). Because such objects are needed in order to fully represent the meaning of a sentence and to assert world knowledge, we introduce **semantic nodes** which are discourse referents of lexical items (whereas frames describe their meanings).

In this paper, we present VigNet, a resource which extends FrameNet to incorporate world and graphical knowledge. We achieve this goal by addressing the three issues above. We first extend frames by adding more information to them (specifically, about decomposition relevant to graphical grounding and more precise selectional restrictions). We call a frame with graphical information a **vignette**. We then extend the structure defined by FrameNet by adding new frames and vignettes, for example for *wash an apple*. The result we call VigNet. Finally, we extend VigNet with a system of nodes which instantiate frames; these nodes we call **semantic nodes**. They get their meaning only from the frames they instantiate. All three extensions are conservative extensions of frames and FrameNet. The semantic theory that VigNet instantiates we call **Vignette Semantics** and we believe it to be a conservative extension (and thus in the spirit of) frame semantics.

This paper is structured as follows. In Section 2, we review frame semantics and FrameNet. Section 3 presents a more detailed description of VigNet, and we provide examples in Section 4. Since VigNet is intended to be used in a large-coverage system, the population of VigNet with knowledge is a crucial issue which we address in Section 5. We discuss related work in Section 6 and conclude in Section 7.

2 Frame Semantics and FrameNet

Frame Semantics (FS; Fillmore (1982)) is based on the idea that the meaning of a word can only be fully understood in context of the entire conceptual structure surrounding it, called the word's frame. When the meaning of a word is evoked in a hearer's mind all related concepts are activated simultaneously and we can rely on this structure to transfer information in a conversation. Frames can describe states-of-affairs, events or complex objects. Each frame contains a set of specific frame elements (FEs), which are labeled semantic argument slots describing participants in the frame. For instance, the word *buy* evokes the frame for a commercial transaction scenario, which includes a buyer and a seller that exchange money for goods. A speaker is aware of what typical buyers, sellers, and goods are. He may also have a mental prototype of the visual scenario itself (e.g. standing at a counter in a store). In FS the role of syntactic theory and the lexicon is to explain how the syntactic dependents of a word that realizes a frame (i.e. arguments and adjuncts) are mapped to frame elements via valence patterns.

FrameNet (FN; Baker et al. (1998), Ruppenhofer et al. (2010)) is a lexical resource based on FS. Frames in FN (around 1000) [1] are defined in terms of their frame elements, relations to other frames and semantic types of FEs. Beyond this, the meaning of the frame (how the FEs are related to each other) is only described in natural language. FN contains about 11,800 lexical units, which are pairings of words and frames. These come with annotated example sentences (about 150,000) to illustrate their valence patterns. FN contains a network of directed frame-to-frame relations. In the INHERITANCE relation a child-frame inherits all semantic properties from the superframe. The frame relations SUBFRAME and PRECEDES refer to sub-events and events following in temporal order respectively. The parent frame's FEs are mapped to the child's FEs. For instance CAUSE_TO_WAKE inherits from TRANSITIVE_ACTION and its sleeper FE maps to agent. Other relations include PERSPECTIVE_ON, CAUSATIVE_OF, and INCHOATIVE_OF. Frame relations captures important semantic facts about frames. For instance the hierarchical organization of INHERITANCE allows to view an event on varying levels of specificity. Finally, FN contains a small ontology of semantic types for frame elements, which can be interpreted as selectional restrictions (e.g. an agent frame element must be filled by a **sentient** being).

3 Vignette Semantics

In Section 1, we motivated VigNet by the need for a resource that allows us to relate language to a grounded semantics, where for us the graphical representation is a stand-in for grounding. We described three reasons for extending FrameNet to VigNet: we need more meaning in a frame, we need more frames and more types of frames, and we need to instantiate frames in a clean manner. We discuss these refinements in more detail in this section.

[1] Numbers refer to FrameNet 1.5

- **Vignettes** are frames that are decomposed into graphical primitives and can be visualized. Like other fames they are motivated by frame semantics; they correspond to a conceptual structure evoked by the lexical units which are associated with it.

- VigNet includes individual frames for each (content) lexical item. This provides **finer-grained semantics** than given with FrameNet frames themselves. These lexically-coupled frames leverage the existing structure of their parent frames. For example, the SELF_MOTION frame contains lexical items for *run* and *swim* which have very different meaning even though they share the same frame and FEs (such as SOURCE, GOAL, and PATH). We therefore define frames for RUN and SWIM which inherit from SELF_MOTION. We assume also that frames and lexical items that are missing from FrameNet are defined and linked to the rest of FrameNet as needed.

- Even more specific frames are created to represent **composed vignettes**. These are vignettes that ground meaning in different ways than the primitive vignette that they specialize. The only motivation for their existence is the graphical grounding. For example, we cannot determine how to represent washing an apple from the knowledge of how to represent generic washing and an apple. So we define a new vignette specifically for *washing a small fruit*. From the point of view of lexical semantics, it uses two lexical items (wash and apple) and their interpretation, but for us, since we are interested in grounding, it is a single vignette. Note that it is not necessary to create specific vignettes for every concrete verb/argument combination. Because vignettes are visually inspired relatively few general vignettes (e.g. *manipulate an object on a fixture*) suffices to visualize many possible scenarios.

- A new type of frame-to-frame relation, which we call SUBFRAME-PARALLEL is used to decompose vignettes into a set of more primitive semantic relations between their arguments. Unlike FrameNet's SUBFRAME relation which represents temporally sequential subframes, in SUBFRAME-PARALLEL, the subframes are all active at the same time, provide a conceptual and spatial decomposition of the frame, and can serve as spatial constraints on the frame elements. A frame is called a vignette if it can be decomposed into graphical primitives using SUBFRAME-PARALLEL relations. For instance in the vignette WASH-SMALL-OBJ for *washing a small object in a sink*, the washer has to be in front of the sink. We assert a SUBFRAME-PARALLEL relation between WASH-SMALL-OBJ and FRONTOF, mapping the washer FE to the figure FE and sink to ground.

- FrameNet has a very limited number of semantic types that are used to restrict the values of FEs. Vignette semantics uses **selectional restrictions** to differentiate between vignettes that have the same parent. For example, the vignette invoked for washing a small object in a sink would restrict the semantic type of the theme (the entity being washed) to anything small, or, more generally, to any object that is washed in this way (apples, hard-boiled eggs, etc). The vignette used for washing a vehicle in a driveway with a hose would restrict its theme to some set of large objects or vehicle types. Selectional restrictions are asserted using the same mechanism as decompositions.

- As mentioned in Section 1, in FrameNet annotations frame elements (FEs) are filled with text spans. Therefore, while frame semantics in general is a deep semantic theory, FrameNet annotations only represent shallow semantics and it is not immediately obvious how FrameNet can be used to build a full semantic representations of a sentence. In Vignette semantics, when a frame is evoked by a lexical item, it is *instantiated* as a semantic node. Its FEs are then bound not to subphrases, but to semantic nodes which are the instantiations of the frames evoked by those subphrases.

Section 3.1 investigates semantic nodes in more detail. Section 3.2 illustrates different types of vignettes (objects, actions, locations) and how they are defined using the SUBFRAME_PARALLEL relation. In Section 3.3 we discuss selectional restrictions.

3.1 Semantic Nodes and Relational Knowledge

The intuition behind semantic nodes is that they represent objects, events or situations. They can also represent plurals or generics. For instance we could have semantic node **city**, denoting the class of cities and a semantic node **paris**, that denotes the city Paris. Note that there is also a frame CITY and a frame PARIS that contain the conceptual structure associated with the words *city* and *Paris*. Frames represent the linguistic and the conceptual aspect of knowledge; the intensional *meaning* of a word. They provide knowledge to answer questions such as "What is an apple?" or "How do you wash an apple?". In contrast, semantic nodes are extensional, i.e. *denotations*. They represent the knowledge to answer questions such as "In what season are apples harvested?" or "How did Percy wash that apple just now?".

As mentioned above semantic nodes allow us to build full meaning representations of entire sentences in discourse. Therefore, while frame definitions are fixed, semantic nodes can be added dynamically during discourse understanding or generation to model the instances of frames that language is evoking. We call such nodes **temporary semantic nodes**. They they are closely related to the discourse referents of Discourse Representation Theory (Kamp, 1981) and related concepts in other theories. In contrast, **persistent semantic nodes** are used to store world knowledge which is distinct from the conceptual knowledge encoded within frames and their relations; for example, the frame for *moon* will not encode the fact that the moon's circumference is 6,790 miles, but we may record that using a knowledge based of external assertions semantic nodes are given their meaning by corresponding frames (CIRCUMFERENCE, MILE, etc.). A temporary semantic node can become persistent by being retained in the knowledge base.

3.2 Vignette Types and their Decomposition

A vignette is a frame in the FrameNet sense that is decomposed to a set of more primitive frames using the SUBFRAME-PARALLEL frame-to-frame relation. The frame elements (FEs) of a vignette are defined as in FrameNet, except that our grounding in the graphical representation gives us a new, strong criterion to choose what the FEs are: they are the objects necessarily involved in the visual scene associated with that vignette. The subframes represent the spatial and other relations between the FEs. The resulting semantic relations specify how the scene elements are spatially arranged. This mechanism covers several different cases.

For **actions**, we conceptually freeze the action in time, much as in a comic book panel, and represent it in a vignette with a set of objects, spatial relations between those objects, and poses characteristic for the humans (and other pliable beings) involved in that action. Action vignettes will typically be specialized to composed vignettes, so that the applicability of different vignettes with the same parent frame will depend on the values of the FEs of the parent. In the process of creating composed vignettes, FEs are often added because additional objects are required to play auxiliary roles. As a result, the FEs of an action vignette are the union of the semantic roles of the important participants and props involved in that enactment of the action with the FEs of the parent frame. For instance the following vignette describes one concrete way of *washing a small fruit*. Note that we have included a new FE sink which is not motivated in the frame WASH.[2] Note also that this vignette also contains a selectional restriction on its theme, which we will discuss in the next subsection and which is not shown here.

WASH-SMALL-FRUIT(washer, theme, sink)
FRONTOF(figure:washer, figure:sink)
FACING(figure:washer, figure:sink)
GRASP(grasper:washer, theme:theme)
REACH(reacher:washer, target:sink)

In this notation the head row contains the vignette name and its FEs in parentheses. For readability we will often omit FEs that are part of the vignette but not restricted or used in any mentioned relation. The lower box contains the vignette decomposition and implicitly specifies SUBFRAME-PARALLEL frame-to-frame relations. In the decomposition of a vignette V we use the notation F(a:b, $\cdots$) to indicate that the FE a of frame F is mapped to the FE b of V. When V is instantiated the semantic node binding to a must also be able to bind to b in F.

Locations are represented by vignettes which express constraints between a set of objects characteristic for the given location. The FEs of location vignettes include these constituent objects. For example, one type of living room (of many possible ones) might contain a couch, a coffee table, and a fireplace in a certain arrangement.

LIVING-ROOM_42(left_wall, far_wall, couch, coffee_table, fireplace)
TOUCHING(figure:couch, ground:left_wall)
FACING(figure:couch, ground:right_wall)
FRONTOF(figure:coffee_table, ground: sofa)
EMBEDDED(figure:fire-place, ground:far_wall)

Even ordinary **physical objects** will have certain characteristic parts with size, shape, and spatial relations that can be expressed by vignettes. For example, an object type such as a kind of *stop sign* can be defined as a two-foot-wide, red, hexagonal metal sheet displaying the word "STOP" positioned on the top of a 6 foot high post.

STOP-SIGN(sign-part, post-part, texture)
MATERIAL(theme:sign-part, material:METAL)
MATERIAL(theme:post-part, material:METAL)
DIAMETER(theme:sign-part, diameter:**2 feet**)
HEIGHT(theme:post-part, height:**6 feet**)
ONTOP(figure:sign-part, ground:post-part)
TEXTURE(theme:sign-part, texture:***"STOP"***)

In addition, many real-world objects do not correspond to lexical items but are elaborations on them or combinations. These **sublexical entities** can be represented by vignettes as well. For example, one such 3D object in our text-to-scene system is a goat head mounted on a piece of wood. This object is represented by a vignette with two FEs (ghead, gwood) representing the goat's head and the wood. The vignette decomposes into ON(ghead, gwood).

While there can be many vignettes for a single lexical item, representing the many ways a location, action, or object can be constituted, vignettes need not be specialized for every particular situation and can be more or less general. In one exteme creating vignettes for every verb/argument combination would clearly lead to a combinatorial explosion and is not feasible. In the other extreme we can define rather general vignettes. For example, a vignette

[2]FrameNet does not currently contain a WASH frame, but if it did, it would not contain an FE sink.

USE-TOOL for using a tool on a theme can be represented by the user GRASPING the tool and REACHING towards the theme. These vignettes can be used in decompositions of more concrete vignettes (e.g. HAMMER-NAIL-INTO-WALL). They can also be used directly if no other more concrete vignette can be applied (because it does not exist or its selectional restrictions cannot be satisfied). In this way by defining a small set of such vignettes we can visualize approximate scenes for a large number of descriptions.

3.3 Selectional Restrictions on Frame Elements

To define a frame we need to specify selectional restrictions on the semantic type of its FEs. Instead of relying on a fixed inventory of semantic types, we assert conceptual knowledge and external assertions over persistent semantic types. This allows us to use VigNet's large set of frames to represent such knowledge. For example, an *apple* can be defined as a small round fruit.

APPLE(self)
SHAPEOF(figure:self, shape:**spherical**) SIZEOF(figure:self, size:**small**)

APPLE is simply a frame that contains a self FE, which allows us to make assertions about the concept (i.e. about any semantic node bound to the self FE). Frame elements of this type are not unusual in FrameNet, where they are mainly used for frames containing common nouns (for instance the Substance FE contains a substance FE). In VigNet we implicitly use self in all frames, including frames describing situations and events.

We use the same mechanism to define specialized compound vignettes such as WASH_SMALL_FRUIT. We extend WASH in the following way to restrict it to small fruits (we abreviate F(self:a) as a=F for readability).

WASH-SMALL-FRUIT(washer, theme, sink)
% selectional restrictions sink=SINK, washer=PERSON, theme=x, x=FRUIT, SIZEOF(figure:x,size:**small**)
% decomposition FRONTOF(figure:washer, figure:sink) FACING(figure:washer, figure:sink) GRASP(grasper:washer, theme:theme) REACH(reacher:washer, target:sink)

4 Examples

In this section we give further examples of visual action vignettes for the verb *wash*. The selectional restrictions and graphical decomposition of these vignettes vary depending on the type of object being washed. The first example shows a vignette for *washing a vehicle*.

WASH-VEHICLE(washer, theme, instr, location)
washer=PERSON, theme=VEHICLE, instr=HOSE, location=DRIVEWAY
ONSURFACE(figure:theme, ground:location) FRONTOF(figure:washer, ground:theme) FACING(figure:washer, ground:theme) GRASP(grasper:washer, theme:instrument) AIM(aimer:washer, theme:instr, target:theme)

The following two vignettes represent a case where the object being washed alone does not determine which vignette to apply. If the instrument is unspecified one or the other could be used. We illustrate one option in figure 1 (right).

WASH-FLOOR-W-SPONGE(washer,theme,instr)
washer=PERSON, theme=FLOOR, instr=SPONGE
KNEELING(agent:washer), GRASP(grasper:washer, theme:instr), REACH(reacher:washer, target:theme)

WASH-FLOOR-W-MOP(washer, theme, instr)
washer=PERSON, theme=FLOOR, instr=MOP
GRASP(grasper:washer, theme:instr), REACHWITH(reacher:washer, target:theme, instr:instr)

It is easy to come up with other concrete vignettes for *wash* (washing windows, babies, hands, dishes...). As mentioned in section 3.2 more general vignettes can be defined for very broad object classes. In choosing vignettes, the most specific will be used (looking at type matching hierarchies), so general vignettes will only be chosen when more specific ones are unavailable. The following generic vignette describes *washing any large object*.

WASH-LARGE-OBJECT(washer, theme instrument)
washer=PERSON, theme=OBJECT, instrument=SPONGE, SIZEOF(figure:theme, size:**large**)
FACING(figure:washer, ground:theme) GRASP(grasper:washer, theme:instrument) REACH(reacher:washer, target:theme)

In our final example, a vignette for *picking fruit* uses the following assertion of world knowledge about particular types of fruit and the trees they come from:
SOURCE-OF(theme:x, source:y), APPLE(self:x), APPLETREE(self:y)
In matching the vignette to the verb frame and its arguments, the source frame element is bound to the type of tree for the given theme (fruit).

PICK-FRUIT(picker, theme, source)
picker=PERSON, theme=FRUIT, source=TREE, SOURCEOF(theme:theme, source:source)
UNDERCANOPY(figure:picker, canopy:source) GRASP(grasper:picker, theme:theme) REACH(reacher:picker, target:source.branch)

5 VigNet

We are developing VigNet as a general purpose resource, but with the specific goal of using it in text-to-scene generation. In this section we first describe various methods to populate VigNet. We then sketch how we create graphical representations from VigNet meaning representations.

5.1 Populating VigNet

VigNet is being populated using several approaches:

- Amazon Mechanical Turk is being used to acquire scene elements for location and action vignettes as well as the spatial relations among those elements. For locations, Turkers are shown representative pictures of different locations as well as variants of similar locations, thereby providing distinct vignettes for each location. We also use Mechanical Turk to acquire general purpose relational information for objects and actions such as default locations, materials, contents, and parts.

- We extract relations such as typical locations for actions from corpora based on co-occurance patterns of location and action terms. This is based on ideas described in (Sproat, 2001). We also rely on corpora to induce new lexical units and selectional preferences.

- A large set of semantic nodes and frames for nouns has been imported from the noun lexicon of the WordsEye text-to-scene system (Coyne and Sproat, 2001). This lexicon currently contains 15,000 lexical items and is tied to a library of 2,200 3D objects and 10,000 images Semantic relations between these nodes include parthood, containment, size, style (e.g. antique or modern), overall shape, material, as well as spatial tags denoting important spatial regions on the object. We also import graphically-oriented vignettes from WordsEye. These are used to capture the meaning of sub-lexical 3D objects such as the mounted goat head described earlier.

- Finally, we intend to use WordsEye itself to allow users to visualize vignettes as they define them, as a way to improve vignette accuracy and relevancy to the actual use of the system.

While the population of VigNet is not the focus of this paper, it is our goal to create a usable resource that can be populated with a reasonable amount of effort. We note that opposed to resources like FrameNet that require skilled lexicographers, we only need simple visual annotation that can easily be done by untrained Mechanical Turkers. In addition, as described in section 3.2, vignettes defined at more abstract levels of the frame hierarchy can be used and composed to cover large numbers of frames in a plausible manner. This allows more specific vignettes to be defined where the differences are most significant. VigNet is is focused on visually-oriented language involving tangible objects. However, abstract, process-oriented language and relations such as negation can be depicted iconically with general vignettes. Examples of these can be seen in the figurative and metaphorical depictions shown in (Coyne and Sproat, 2001).

5.2 Using VigNet in Text-to-Scene Generation

To compose a scene from text input such as *the man is washing the apple* it is necessary to parse the sentence into a semantic representation (evoking frames for each content word) and to then resolve the language-level semantics to a set of graphical entities and relations. To create a low-level graphical representation all frame elements need to be filled with appropriate semantic nodes. Frames support the selection of these nodes by specifying constraints on them using selectional restrictions. The

SUBFRAME-PARALLEL decomposition of vignettes then ultimately relates these nodes using elementary spatial vignettes (FRONTOF, ON, ...).

Note that it is possible to describe scenes directly using these vignettes (such as *The man is in front of the sink. He is holding an apple.*), as was used to create the mock-ups in figure 1.

Vignettes can be directly applied or composed together. Composing vignettes involves unifying their frame elements. For example, in washing an apple, the WASH-SMALL-FRUIT vignette uses a sink. From world knowledge we know (via instances of the TYPICAL-LOCATION frame) that washing food typically takes place in the KITCHEN. To create a scene we compose the two vignettes together by unifying the sink in the location vignette with the sink in the action vignette.

6 Related Work

The grounding of natural language to graphical relations has been investigated in very early text-to-scene systems (Boberg, 1972), (Simmons, 1975), (Kahn, 1979), (Adorni et al., 1984), and then later in Put (Clay and Wilhelms, 1996), and WordsEye (Coyne and Sproat, 2001). Other systems, such as CarSim (Dupuy et al., 2001), Jack (Badler et al., 1998), and CONFUCIUS (Ma and McKevitt, 2006) target animation and virtual environments rather than scene construction. A graphically grounded lexical-semantic resource such as VigNet would be of use to these and related domains. The concept of vignettes as graphical realizations of more general frames was introduced in (Coyne et al., 2010).

In addition to FrameNet, much work has been done in developing theories and resources for lexical semantics and common-sense knowledge. VerbNet (Kipper et al., 2000) focuses on verb subcat patterns grouped by Levin verb classes (Levin, 1993), but also grounds verb semantics into a small number of causal primitives representing temporal constraints tied to causality and state changes. VerbNet lacks the ability to compose semantic constraints or use arbitrary semantic relations in those constraints. Conceptual Dependency theory (Schank and Abelson, 1977) specifies a small number of state-change primitives into which all verbs are reduced. Event Logic (Siskind, 1995) decomposes actions into intervals describing state changes and allows visual grounding by specifying truth conditions for a small set of spatial primitives (a similar formalism is used by Ma and McKevitt (2006)). (Bailey et al., 1998) and related work proposes a representation in many ways similar to ours, in which lexical items are paired with a detailed specification of actions in terms of elementary body poses and movements. In contrast to these temporally-oriented approaches, VigNet grounds semantics in spatial constraints active at a single moment in time. This allows for and emphasizes *contextual reasoning* rather than causal reasoning. In addition, VigNet emphasizes a holistic frame semantic perspective, rather than emphasizing decomposition alone. Several resources for common-sense knowledge exist or have been proposed. In OpenMind and ConceptNet (Havasi et al., 2007) online crowd-sourcing is used to collect a large set of common-sense assertions. These assertions are normalized into a set of a couple dozen relations. The Cyc project is using the web to augment its large ontology and knowledge base of common sense knowledge (Matuszek et al., 2005). PRAXICON (Pastra, 2008) is a grounded conceptual resources that integrates motor-sensoric, visual, pragmatic and lexical knowledge (via WordNet). It targets the embodied robotics community and does not directly focus on scene generation. It also focuses on individual lexical items, while VigNet, like FrameNet, takes syntactic context into account.

7 Conclusion

We have described a new semantic paradigm that we call vignette semantics. Vignettes are extensions of FrameNet frames and represent the specific ways in which semantic frames can be realized in the world. Mapping frames to vignettes involves translating between high-level frame semantics and the lower-level relations used to compose a scene. Knowledge about objects, both in terms of their semantic types and the affordances they provide is used to make that translation. FrameNet frames, coupled with semantic nodes representing entity classes, provide a powerful relational framework to express such knowledge. We are developing a new resource VigNet which will implement this framework and be used in our text-to-scene generation system.

References

G. Adorni, M. Di Manzo, and F. Giunchiglia. 1984. Natural Language Driven Image Generation. In *Proceedings of COLING 1984*, pages 495–500, Stanford, CA.

N. Badler, R. Bindiganavale, J. Bourne, M. Palmer, J. Shi, and W. Schule. 1998. A parameterized action representation for virtual human agents. In *Workshop on Embodied Conversational Characters*, Tahoe City, CA.

D. Bailey, N. Chang, J. Feldman, and S. Narayanan. 1998. Extending Embodied Lexical Development. In *Proceedings of the Annual Meeting of the Cognitive Science Society*, Madison, WI.

C. Baker, C. Fillmore, and J. Lowe. 1998. The Berkeley Framenet Project. In *Proceedings of COLING 1998*, pages 86–90.

R. Boberg. 1972. Generating line drawings from abstract scene descriptions. Master's thesis, Dept. of Elec. Eng, MIT, Cambridge, MA.

S. R. Clay and J. Wilhelms. 1996. Put: Language-based interactive manipulation of objects. *IEEE Computer Graphics and Applications*, 16(2):31–39.

B. Coyne and R. Sproat. 2001. WordsEye: An automatic text-to-scene conversion system. In *Proceedings of the Annual Conference on Computer Graphics*, pages 487–496, Los Angeles, CA.

B. Coyne, O. Rambow, J. Hirschberg, and R. Sproat. 2010. Frame Semantics in Text-to-Scene Generation. In *Proceedings of the KES'10 workshop on 3D Visualisation of Natural Language*, Cardiff, Wales.

S. Dupuy, A. Egges, V. Legendre, and P. Nugues. 2001. Generating a 3D Simulation Of a Car Accident from a Written Description in Natural Language: The CarSim System. In *Proceedings of ACL Workshop on Temporal and Spatial Information Processing*, pages 1–8, Toulouse, France.

C. J. Fillmore. 1982. Frame semantics. In Linguistic Society of Korea, editor, *Linguistics in the Morning Calm*, pages 111–137. Hanshin Publishing Company, Seoul.

C. Havasi, R. Speer, and J. Alonso. 2007. ConceptNet 3: a Flexible, Multilingual Semantic Network for Common Sense Knowledge. In *Proceedings of RANLP 2007*, Borovets, Bulgaria.

K. Kahn. 1979. *Creation of Computer Animation from Story Descriptions*. Ph.D. thesis, MIT, AI Lab, Cambridge, MA.

H. Kamp. 1981. A Theory of Truth and Semantic Representation. In Groenendijk, J. and Janssen, T. and Stokhof, M., editor, *Formal Methods in the Study of Language*, pages 277–322. de Gruyter, Amsterdam.

K. Kipper, H. T. Dang, and M. Palmer. 2000. Class-Based Construction of a Verb Lexicon. In *Proceedings of AAAI 2000*, Austin, TX.

B. Levin. 1993. *English verb classes and alternations: a preliminary investigation*. University Of Chicago Press.

M. Ma and P. McKevitt. 2006. Virtual human animation in natural language visualisation. *Artificial Intelligence Review*, 25:37–53, April.

C. Matuszek, M. Witbrock, R. C. Kahlert, J. Cabral, D. Schneider, P. Shah, and D. Lenat. 2005. Searching for Common Sense: Populating Cyc from the Web. In *Proceedings of AAAI 2005*, pages 1430–1435, Pittsburgh, PA.

K. Pastra. 2008. PRAXICON: The Development of a Grounding Resource. In *Proceedings of the International Workshop on Human-Computer Conversation*, Bellagio, Italy.

J. Ruppenhofer, M. Ellsworth, M. Petruck, C. R. Johnson, and J. Scheffczyk. 2010. *Framenet II: Extended Theory and Practice*. ICSI Berkeley.

R. C. Schank and R. Abelson. 1977. *Scripts, Plans, Goals, and Understanding*. Earlbaum, Hillsdale, NJ.

R. Simmons. 1975. The CLOWNS Microworld. In *Proceedings of the Workshop on Theoretical Issues in Natural Language Processing*, pages 17–19, Cambridge, MA.

J. M. Siskind. 1995. Grounding language in perception. *Artificial Intelligence Review*, 8:371–391.

R. Sproat. 2001. Inferring the environment in a text-to-scene conversion system. In *International Conference on Knowledge Capture*, Victoria, BC.

Transition-based Semantic Role Labeling Using Predicate Argument Clustering

Jinho D. Choi
Department of Computer Science
University of Colorado at Boulder
choijd@colorado.edu

Martha Palmer
Department of Linguistics
University of Colorado at Boulder
mpalmer@colorado.edu

Abstract

This paper suggests two ways of improving semantic role labeling (SRL). First, we introduce a novel transition-based SRL algorithm that gives a quite different approach to SRL. Our algorithm is inspired by shift-reduce parsing and brings the advantages of the transition-based approach to SRL. Second, we present a self-learning clustering technique that effectively improves labeling accuracy in the test domain. For better generalization of the statistical models, we cluster verb predicates by comparing their predicate argument structures and apply the clustering information to the final labeling decisions. All approaches are evaluated on the CoNLL'09 English data. The new algorithm shows comparable results to another state-of-the-art system. The clustering technique improves labeling accuracy for both in-domain and out-of-domain tasks.

1 Introduction

Semantic role labeling (SRL) has sparked much interest in NLP (Shen and Lapata, 2007; Liu and Gildea, 2010). Lately, dependency-based SRL has shown advantages over constituent-based SRL (Johansson and Nugues, 2008). Two main benefits can be found. First, dependency parsing is much faster than constituent parsing, whereas constituent parsing is usually considered to be a bottleneck to SRL in terms of execution time. Second, dependency structure is more similar to predicate argument structure than phrase structure because it specifically defines relations between a predicate and its arguments with labeled arcs. Unlike constituent-based SRL that maps phrases to semantic roles, dependency-based SRL maps headwords to semantic roles because there is no phrasal node in dependency structure. This may lead to a concern about getting the actual semantic chunks back, but Choi and Palmer (2010) have shown that it is possible to recover the original chunks from the headwords with minimal loss, using a certain type of dependency structure.

Traditionally, either constituent or dependency-based, semantic role labeling is done in two steps, argument identification and classification (Gildea and Jurafsky, 2002). This is from a general belief that each step requires a different set of features (Xue and Palmer, 2004), and training these steps in a pipeline takes less time than training them as a joint-inference task. However, recent machine learning algorithms can deal with large scale vector spaces without taking too much training time (Hsieh et al., 2008). Furthermore, from our experience in dependency parsing, handling these steps together improves accuracy in identification as well as classification (unlabeled and labeled attachment scores in dependency parsing). This motivates the development of a new semantic role labeling algorithm that treats these two steps as a joint inference task.

Our algorithm is inspired by shift-reduce parsing (Nivre, 2008). The algorithm uses several transitions to identify predicates and their arguments with semantic roles. One big advantage of the transition-based approach is that it can use previously identified arguments as features to predict the next argument. We apply this technique to our approach and achieve comparable results to another state-of-the-art system evaluated on the same data sets.

NO-PRED	$(\lambda_1, \lambda_2, j, \lambda_3, [i\|\lambda_4], A) \Rightarrow ([\lambda_1\|j], \lambda_2, i, \lambda_3, \lambda_4, A)$ $\exists j.\ \text{oracle}(j) \neq \text{predicate}$
SHIFT	$(\lambda_1, \lambda_2, j, [i\|\lambda_3], \lambda_4, A) \Rightarrow ([\lambda_2\|j], [\,], i, [\,], \lambda_3, A)$ $\exists j.\ \text{oracle}(j) = \text{predicate} \quad \wedge \quad \lambda_1 = [\,] \quad \wedge \quad \lambda_4 = [\,]$
NO-ARC$^{\leftarrow}$	$([\lambda_1\|i], \lambda_2, j, \lambda_3, \lambda_4, A) \Rightarrow (\lambda_1, [i\|\lambda_2], j, \lambda_3, \lambda_4, A)$ $\exists j.\ \text{oracle}(j) = \text{predicate} \quad \wedge \quad \exists i.\text{oracle}(i,j) = \{i \not\leftarrow j\}$
NO-ARC$^{\rightarrow}$	$(\lambda_1, \lambda_2, j, \lambda_3, [i\|\lambda_4], A) \Rightarrow (\lambda_1, \lambda_2, j, [\lambda_3\|i], \lambda_4, A)$ $\exists j.\ \text{oracle}(j) = \text{predicate} \quad \wedge \quad \exists i.\text{oracle}(i,j) = \{j \not\rightarrow i\}$
LEFT-ARC$^{\leftarrow}_{\text{L}}$	$([\lambda_1\|i], \lambda_2, j, \lambda_3, \lambda_4, A) \Rightarrow (\lambda_1, [i\|\lambda_2], j, \lambda_3, \lambda_4, A \cup \{i \overset{\text{L}}{\leftarrow} j\})$ $\exists j.\ \text{oracle}(j) = \text{predicate} \quad \wedge \quad \exists i.\text{oracle}(i,j) = \{i \overset{\text{L}}{\leftarrow} j\}$
RIGHT-ARC$^{\rightarrow}_{\text{L}}$	$(\lambda_1, \lambda_2, j, \lambda_3, [i\|\lambda_4], A) \Rightarrow (\lambda_1, \lambda_2, j, [\lambda_3\|i], \lambda_4, A \cup \{j \overset{\text{L}}{\rightarrow} i\})$ $\exists j.\ \text{oracle}(j) = \text{predicate} \quad \wedge \quad \exists i.\text{oracle}(i,j) = \{j \overset{\text{L}}{\rightarrow} i\}$

Table 1: Transitions in our bidirectional top-down search algorithm. For each row, the first line shows a transition and the second line shows preconditions of the transition.

For better generalization of the statistical models, we apply a self-learning clustering technique. We first cluster predicates in test data using automatically generated predicate argument structures, then cluster predicates in training data by using the previously found clusters as seeds. Our experiments show that this technique improves labeling accuracy for both in-domain and out-of-domain tasks.

2 Transition-based semantic role labeling

Dependency-based semantic role labeling can be viewed as a special kind of dependency parsing in the sense that both try to find relations between word pairs. However, they are distinguished in two major ways. First, unlike dependency parsing that tries to find some kind of relation between any word pair, semantic role labeling restricts its search only to top-down relations between predicate and argument pairs. Second, dependency parsing requires one head for each word, so the final output is a tree, whereas semantic role labeling allows multiple predicates for each argument. Thus, not all dependency parsing algorithms, such as a maximum spanning tree algorithm (Mcdonald and Pereira, 2006), can be naively applied to semantic role labeling.

Some transition-based dependency parsing algorithms have been adapted to semantic role labeling and shown good results (Henderson et al., 2008; Titov et al., 2009). However, these algorithms are originally designed for dependency parsing, so are not necessarily customized for semantic role labeling. Here, we present a novel transition-based algorithm dedicated to semantic role labeling. The key difference between this algorithm and most other transition-based algorithms is in its directionality. Given an identified predicate, this algorithm tries to find top-down relations between the predicate and the words on both left and right-hand sides, whereas other transition-based algorithms would consider words on either the left or the right-hand side, but not both. This bidirectional top-down search makes more sense for semantic role labeling because predicates are always assumed to be the heads of their arguments, an assumption that cannot be generalized to dependency parsing, and arguments can appear either side of the predicate.

Table 1 shows transitions used in our algorithm. All parsing states are represented as tuples (λ_1, λ_2, p, λ_3, λ_4, A), where $\lambda_{1..4}$ are lists of word indices and p is either a word index of the current predicate candidate or $\nexists$ indicating no predicate candidate. $\lambda_{1,4}$ contain indices to be compared with p and $\lambda_{2,3}$ contain indices already compared with p. A is a set of labeled arcs representing previously identified arguments with respect to their predicates. $\leftarrow$ and $\rightarrow$ indicate parsing directions. L is a semantic role label, and i, j represent indices of their corresponding word tokens. The initial state is ([ ], [ ], 1, [ ], $[2, \ldots, n]$, $\emptyset$), where w_1 and w_n are the first and the last words in a sentence, respectively. The final state is (λ_1, λ_2, $\nexists$, [ ], [ ], A), i.e., the algorithm terminates when there is no more predicate candidate left.

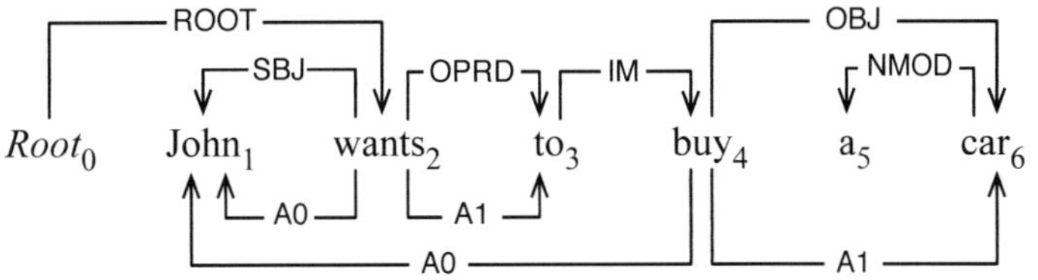

Figure 1: An example of a dependency tree with semantic roles. The upper and lower arcs stand for syntactic and semantic dependencies, respectively. `SBJ`, `OBJ`, `OPRD`, `IM`, `NMOD` stand for a subject, object, object predicative, infinitive marker, and noun-modifier. `A0`, `A1` stand for `ARG0`, `ARG1` in PropBank (Palmer et al., 2005).

	Transition	λ_1	λ_2	p	λ_3	λ_4	A
0		[ ]	[ ]	1	[ ]	[2..6]	$\emptyset$
1	NO-PRED	[1]	[ ]	2	[ ]	[3..6]	
2	LEFT-ARC	[ ]	[1]	2	[ ]	[3..6]	$A \cup \{1 \leftarrow\text{A0}- 2\}$
3	RIGHT-ARC	[ ]	[1]	2	[3]	[4..6]	$A \cup \{2 -\text{A1}\rightarrow 3\}$
4	NO-ARC	[ ]	[1]	2	[3..4]	[5..6]	
5	NO-ARC	[ ]	[1]	2	[3..5]	[6]	
6	NO-ARC	[ ]	[1]	2	[3..6]	[ ]	
7	SHIFT	[1..2]	[ ]	3	[ ]	[4..6]	
8	NO-PRED	[1..3]	[ ]	4	[ ]	[5..6]	
9	NO-ARC	[1..2]	[3]	4	[ ]	[5..6]	
10	NO-ARC	[1]	[2..3]	4	[ ]	[5..6]	
11	LEFT-ARC	[ ]	[1..3]	4	[ ]	[5..6]	$A \cup \{1 \leftarrow\text{A0}- 4\}$
12	NO-ARC	[ ]	[1..3]	4	[5]	[6]	
13	RIGHT-ARC	[ ]	[1..3]	4	[5..6]	[ ]	$A \cup \{4 -\text{A1}\rightarrow 6\}$
14	SHIFT	[1..4]	[ ]	5	[ ]	[6]	
15	NO-PRED	[1..5]	[ ]	6	[ ]	[ ]	
16	NO-PRED	[1..6]	[ ]	$\nexists$	[ ]	[ ]	

Table 2: Parsing states generated by our algorithm for the example in Figure 1.

The algorithm uses six kinds of transitions. NO-PRED is performed when an oracle identifies w_j as not a predicate. All other transitions are performed when w_j is identified as a predicate. SHIFT is performed when both λ_1 and λ_4 are empty, meaning that there are no more argument candidates left for the predicate w_j. NO-ARC is performed when w_i is identified as not an argument of w_j. LEFT-ARC$_\text{L}$ and RIGHT-ARC$_\text{L}$ are performed when w_i is identified as an argument of w_j with a label L. These transitions can be performed in any order as long as their preconditions are satisfied. For our experiments, we use the following generalized sequence:

$$[\ (\text{NO-PRED})* \Rightarrow (\text{LEFT-ARC}_\text{L}^{\leftarrow}|\text{NO-ARC}^{\leftarrow})* \Rightarrow (\text{RIGHT-ARC}_\text{L}^{\rightarrow}|\text{NO-ARC}^{\rightarrow})* \Rightarrow \text{SHIFT}\ ]*$$

Notice that this algorithm does not take separate steps for argument identification and classification. By adding the NO-ARC transitions, we successfully merge these two steps together without decrease in labeling accuracy.[1] Since each word can be a predicate candidate and each predicate considers all other words as argument candidates, a worst-case complexity of the algorithm is $O(n^2)$. To reduce the complexity, Zhao et al. (2009) reformulated a pruning algorithm introduced by Xue and Palmer (2004) for dependency structure by considering only direct dependents of a predicate and its ancestors as argument candidates. This pruning algorithm can be easily applied to our algorithm: the oracle can prefilter such dependents and uses the information to perform NO-ARC transitions without consulting statistical models.

[1] We also experimented with the traditional approach of building separate classifiers for identification and classification, which did not lead to better performance in our case.

Table 2 shows parsing states generated by our algorithm. Our experiments show that this algorithm gives comparable results against another state-of-the-art system.

3 Predicate argument clustering

Some studies showed that verb clustering information could improve performance in semantic role labeling (Gildea and Jurafsky, 2002; Pradhan et al., 2008). This is because semantic role labelers usually perform worse on verbs not seen during training, for which the clustering information can provide useful features. Most previous studies used either bag-of-words or syntactic structure to cluster verbs; however, this may or may not capture the nature of predicate argument structure, which is more semantically oriented. Thus, it is preferable to cluster verbs by their predicate argument structures to get optimized features for semantic role labeling.

In this section, we present a self-learning clustering technique that effectively improves labeling accuracy in the test domain. First, we perform semantic role labeling on the test data using the algorithm in Section 2. Next, we cluster verbs in the test data using predicate argument structures generated by our semantic role labeler (Section 3.2). Then, we cluster verbs in the training data using the verb clusters we found in the test data (Section 3.3). Finally, we re-run our semantic role labeler on the test data using the clustering information. Our experiments show that this technique gives improvement to labeling accuracy for both in and out-of domain tasks.

3.1 Projecting predicate argument structure into vector space

Before clustering, we need to project the predicate argument structure of each verb into vector space. Two kinds of features are used to represent these vectors: semantic role labels and joined tags of semantic role labels and their corresponding word lemmas. Figure 2 shows vector representations of predicate argument structures of verbs, *want* and *buy*, in Figure 1.

Initially, all existing and non-existing features are assigned with a value of 1 and 0, respectively. However, assigning equal values to all existing features is not necessarily fair because some features have higher confidence, or are more important than the others; e.g., `ARG0` and `ARG1` are generally predicted with higher confidence than modifiers, nouns give more important information than some other grammatical categories, etc. Instead, we assign each existing feature with a value computed by the following equations:

Verb	A0	A1	...	john:A0	to:A1	car:A1	...
want	1	1	0s	1	1	0	0s
buy	1	1	0s	1	0	1	0s

Figure 2: Projecting the predicate argument structure of each verb into vector space.

$$s(l_j|v_i) = \frac{1}{1 + exp(-score(l_j|v_i))}$$

$$s(m_j, l_j) = \begin{cases} 1 & (w_j \neq \text{noun}) \\ exp(\frac{count(m_j,l_j)}{\sum_{\forall k} count(m_k,l_k)}) & \end{cases}$$

v_i is the current verb, l_j is the j'th label of v_i, and m_j is l_j's corresponding lemma. $score(l_j|v_i)$ is a score of l_j being a correct argument label of v_i; this is always 1 for training data and is provided by our statistical models for test data. Thus, $s(l_j|v_i)$ is an approximated probability of l_j being a correct argument label of v_i, estimated by the logistic function. $s(m_j, l_j)$ is equal to 1 if w_j is not a noun. If w_j is a noun, it gets a value ≥ 1 given a maximum likelihood of m_j being co-occurred with l_j.[2]

With the vector representation, we can apply any kind of clustering algorithm (Hofmann and Puzicha, 1998; Kamvar et al., 2002). For our experiments, we use k-best hierarchical clustering for test data, and k-means clustering for training data.

3.2 Clustering verbs in test data

Given automatically generated predicate argument structures in the test data, we apply k-best hierarchical clustering; that is, a relaxation of classical hierarchical agglomerative clustering (from now on, HAC; Ward (1963)), to find verb clusters. Unlike HAC that merges a pair of clusters at each iteration, k-best hierarchical clustering merges k-best pairs at

[2]Assigning different weights for nouns resulted in more meaningful clusters in our experiments. We will explore additional grammatical category specific weighting schemes in future work.

each iteration (Lo et al., 2009). Instead of merging a fixed number of k-clusters, we use a threshold to dynamically determine the top k-clusters. Our studies indicate that this technique produces almost as fine-grained clusters as HAC, yet converges much faster.

Our algorithm for k-best hierarchical clustering is presented in Algorithm 1. th_{up} is a threshold that determines which k-best pairs are to be merged (in our case, k_{up} = 0.8). $sim(c_i, c_j)$ is a similarity between clusters c_i and c_j. For our experiments, we use cosine similarity with average-linkage. It is possible that other kinds of similarity metrics would work better, which we will explore as future work. Conditions in line 15 ensure that each cluster is merged with at most one other cluster at each iteration, and conditions in line 17 force at least one cluster to be merged with one other cluster at each iteration. Thus, the algorithm is guaranteed to terminate after at most $(n-1)$ iterations.

When the algorithm terminates, it returns a set of one cluster with different hierarchical levels. For our experiments, we set another threshold, th_{low}, for early break-out: if there is no cluster pair whose similarity is greater than th_{low}, we terminate the algorithm (in our case, th_{low} = 0.7). A cluster set generated by this early break-out contains several unit clusters that are not merged with any other cluster. All of these unit clusters are discarded from the set to improve set quality. This is reasonable because our goal is not to cluster all verbs but to find a useful set of verb clusters that can be mapped to verbs in training data, which can lead to better performance in semantic role labeling.

3.3 Clustering verbs in training data

Given the verb clusters we found in the test data, we search for verbs that are similar to these clusters in the training data. K-means clustering (Hartigan, 1975) is a natural choice for this case because we already know k-number of center clusters to begin with. Each verb in the training data is compared with all verb clusters in the test data, and merged with the cluster that gives the highest similarity. To maintain the quality of the clusters, we use the same threshold, th_{low}, to filter out verbs in the training data that are not similar enough to any verb cluster in the test data. By doing so, we keep only verbs that are more likely to be helpful for semantic role labeling.

input : $C = [c_1, .., c_n]$: c_i is a unit cluster.
$th_{up} \in \mathbb{R}$: threshold.
output: $\hat{C} = [c_1, .., c_m]$: c_j is a unit or merged cluster, where $m \leq n$.

1 **begin**
2 **while** $|C| > 1$ **do**
3 $L \leftarrow list()$
4 **for** $i \in [1, |C| - 1]$ **do**
5 **for** $j \in [i + 1, |C|]$ **do**
6 $t \leftarrow (i, j, sim(c_i, c_j))$
7 $L.add(t)$
8 **end**
9 **end**
10 descendingSortBySimilarity(L)
11 $S \leftarrow set()$
12 **for** $k \in [1, |L|]$ **do**
13 $t \leftarrow L.get(k)$
14 $i \leftarrow t(0); j \leftarrow t(1); sim \leftarrow t(2)$
15 **if** $i \in S$ **or** $j \in S$ **then**
16 **continue**
17 **if** $k = 1$ **or** $sim > th_{up}$ **then**
18 C.add($c_i \cup c_j$); S.add(i, j)
19 C.remove(c_i, c_j)
20 **else**
21 **break**
22 **end**
23 **end**
24 **end**
25 **end**

Algorithm 1: k-best hierarchical clustering.

4 Features

4.1 Baseline features

For a baseline approach, we use features similar to ones used by Johansson and Nugues (2008). All features are assumed to have dependency structures as input. Table 3 shows n-gram feature templates used for our experiments (f: form, m: lemma, p: POS tag, d: dependency label). w_{arg} and w_{pred} are the current argument and predicate candidates. $hd(w)$ stands for the head of w, $lm(w)$, $rm(w)$ stand for the leftmost, rightmost dependents of w, and $ls(w)$, $rs(w)$ stand for the left-nearest, right-nearest siblings of w, with respect to the dependency structures. Some of these features can be presented as a joined feature; e.g., a combination of w_{arg}'s POS tag and lemma.

Word tokens	Features
w_{arg}, w_{pred}	f,m,p,d
$w_{arg\pm1}, hd, lm, rm, ls, rs\ (w_{arg})$	m,p
$w_{pred\pm1}, hd, lm, rm\ (w_{pred})$	m,p

Table 3: N-gram feature templates.

Besides the n-gram features, we use several structural features such as dependency label set, subcategorization, POS path, dependency path, and dependency depth. Dependency label set features are derived by collecting all dependency labels of w_{pred}'s direct dependents. Unlike Johansson and Nugues, we decompose subcategorization features into two parts: one representing the left-hand side and the other representing the right-hand side dependencies of w_{pred}. For the predicate *wants* in Figure 3, we generate $\overleftarrow{\text{SBJ}}$ and $\overrightarrow{\text{OPRD}}$ as separate subcategorization features.

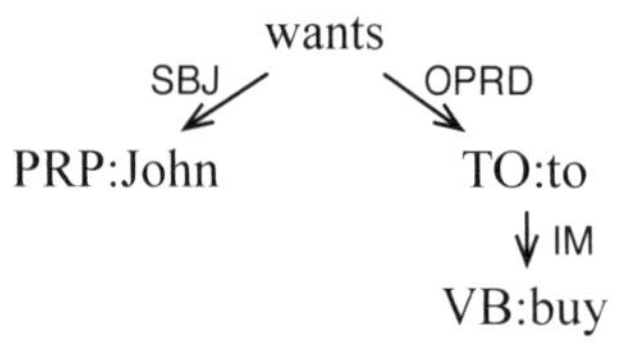

Figure 3: Dependency structure used for subcategorization, path, and depth features.

We also decompose path features into two parts: given the lowest common ancestor (LCA) of w_{arg} and w_{pred}, we generate path features from w_{arg} to the LCA and from the LCA to w_{pred}, separately. For example, the predicate *buy* and the argument *John* in Figure 3 have a LCA at *wants*, so we generate two sets of path features, $\{\uparrow$PRP, $\downarrow$TO$\downarrow$VB$\}$ with POS tags, and $\{\uparrow$SBJ, $\downarrow$OPRD$\downarrow$IM$\}$ with dependency labels. Such decompositions allow more generalization of those features; even if one part is not matched to the current parsing state, the other part can still participate as a feature. Throughout our experiments, these generalized features give slightly higher labeling accuracy than ungeneralized features although they form a smaller feature space.

In addition, we apply dependency path features to w_{pred}'s highest verb chain, which often shares arguments with the predicate (e.g., *John* is a shared argument of the predicate *buy* and its highest verb chain *wants*). To retrieve the highest verb chain, we apply a simple heuristic presented below. The function `getHighestVerbChain` takes a predicate, `pred`, as input and returns its highest verb chain, `vNode`, as output. If there is no verb chain for the predicate, it returns `null` instead. Note that this heuristic is designed to work with dependency relations and labels described by the CoNLL'09 shared task (Hajič et al., 2009).

```
func getHighestVerbChain(pred)
  vNode = pred;
  regex = "CONJ|COORD|IM|OPRD|VC";

  while (regex.matches(vNode.deprel))
    vNode = vNode.head;

  if (vNode != pred) return vNode;
  else               return null;
```

Dependency depth features are a reduced form of path features. Instead of specifying POS tags or dependency labels, we indicate paths with their depths. For instance, *John* and *buy* in Figure 3 have a dependency depth feature of $\uparrow1\downarrow2$, which implies that the depth between *John* and its LCA (*wants*) is 1, and the depth between the LCA and *buy* is 2.

Finally, we use four kinds of binary features: if w_{arg} is a syntactic head of w_{pred}, if w_{pred} is a syntactic head of w_{arg}, if w_{pred} is a syntactic ancestor of w_{arg}, and if w_{pred}'s verb chain has a subject. Each feature gets a value of 1 if true; otherwise, it gets a value of 0.

4.2 Dynamic and clustering features

All dynamic features are derived by using previously identified arguments. Two kinds of dynamic features are used for our experiments. One is a label of the very last predicted numbered argument of w_{pred}. For instance, the parsing state 3 in Table 2 uses a label `A0` as a feature to make its prediction, $wants \xrightarrow{\text{A1}} to$, and the parsing states 4 to 6 use a label `A1` as a feature to make their predictions, NO-ARC's. With this feature, the oracle can narrow down the scope of expected arguments of w_{pred}. The other is a previously identified argument label of w_{arg}. The existence of this feature implies that w_{arg} is already identified as an argument of some other predicate. For instance, when $w_{arg} = John$ and $w_{pred} = buy$ in Table 2, a label `A0` is used as a feature to make the prediction, $John \xleftarrow{\text{A0}} buy$, because $John$ is already identified as an `A0` of $wants$.

Finally, we use w_{pred}'s cluster ID as a feature. The dynamic and clustering features combine a very small portion of the entire feature set, but still give a fair improvement to labeling accuracy.

5 Experiments

5.1 Corpora

All models are trained on Wall Street Journal sections 2-21 and developed on section 24 using automatically generated lemmas and POS tags, as distributed by the CoNLL'09 shared task (Hajič et al., 2009). CoNLL'09 data contains semantic roles for both verb and noun predicates, for which we use only ones related to verb predicates. Furthermore, we do not include predicate sense classification as a part of our task, which is rather a task of word sense disambiguation than semantic role labeling.

For in-domain and out-of-domain evaluations, WSJ section 23 and the Brown corpus are used, also distributed by CoNLL'09. To retrieve automatically generated dependency trees as input to our semantic role labeler, we train our open source dependency parser, called ClearParser[3], on the training set and run the parser on the evaluation sets. ClearParser uses a transition-based dependency parsing algorithm that gives near state-of-the-art results (Choi and Palmer, 2011), and mirrors our SRL algorithm.

5.2 Statistical models

We use Liblinear L2-L1 SVM for learning; a linear classification algorithm using L2 regularization and L1 loss function. This algorithm is designed to handle large scale data: it assumes the data to be linearly separable so does not use any kind of kernel space (Hsieh et al., 2008). As a result, it significantly reduces training time compared to typical SVM, yet performs accurately. For our experiments, we use the following learning parameters: $c = 0.1$ (cost), $e = 0.2$ (termination criterion), $B = 0$ (bias).

Since predicate identification is already provided in the CoNLL'09 data, we do not train NO-PRED. SHIFT does not need to be trained in general because the preconditions of SHIFT can be checked deterministically without consulting statistical models. NO-ARC$^{\leftarrow}$ and LEFT-ARC$_L^{\leftarrow}$ are trained together using the one-vs-all method as are NO-ARC$^{\rightarrow}$ and RIGHT-ARC$_L^{\rightarrow}$. Even with multi-classifications, it takes less than two minutes for the entire training using Liblinear.

[3] http://code.google.com/p/clearparser/

5.3 Accuracy comparisons

Tables 4 and 5 show accuracy comparisons between three models evaluated on the WSJ and Brown corpora, respectively. 'Baseline' uses the features described in Section 4.1. '+Dynamic' uses all baseline features and the dynamic features described in Section 4.2. '+Cluster' uses all previous features and the clustering feature. Even though our baseline system already has high performance, each model shows an improvement over its previous model (very slight for '+Cluster'). The improvement is greater for the out-of-domain task, implying that the dynamic and clustering features help more on new domains. The differences between 'Baseline' and '+Dynamic' are statistically significant for both in and out-of domain tasks (Wilcoxon signed-rank test, treating each sentence as an individual event, $p \leq 0.025$).

	Task	P	R	F1
Baseline	AI	92.57	88.44	90.46
	AI+AC	87.20	83.31	85.21
+Dynamic	AI	92.38	88.76	90.54
	AI+AC	87.33	83.91	85.59*
+Cluster	AI	92.62	88.90	**90.72**
	AI+AC	87.43	83.92	**85.64**
JN (2008)	AI+AC	88.46	83.55	85.93

Table 4: Labeling accuracies evaluated on the WSJ (P: precision, R: recall, F1: F1-score, all in %). 'AI' and 'AC' stand for argument identification and argument classification, respectively.

	Task	P	R	F1
Baseline	AI	90.96	81.57	86.01
	AI+AC	77.11	69.14	72.91
+Dynamic	AI	90.90	82.25	86.36
	AI+AC	77.41	70.05	73.55*
+Cluster	AI	90.87	82.43	**86.44**
	AI+AC	77.47	70.28	**73.70**
JN (2008)	AI+AC	77.67	69.63	73.43

Table 5: Labeling accuracies evaluated on the Brown.

We also compare our results against another state-of-the-art system. Unfortunately, no other system has been evaluated with our exact environmental settings. However, Johansson and Nugues (2008), who showed state-of-the-art performance in CoNLL'08, evaluated their system with settings very similar to ours. Their task was exactly the same as ours; given predicate identification, they evaluated their dependency-based semantic role labeler for argument identification and classification on the WSJ and Brown corpora, distributed by the CoNLL'05 shared task (Carreras and Màrquez, 2005). Since the CoNLL'05 data was not dependency-based, they applied heuristics to build dependency-based predicate argument structures. Their converted data may appear to be a bit different from the CoNLL'09 data we use (e.g., hyphenated words are tokenized by the hyphens in CoNLL'09 data whereas they are not in CoNLL'05 data), but semantic role annotations on headwords should look very similar.

Johansson and Nugues's results are presented as JN (2008) in Tables 4 and 5. Our final system shows comparable results against this system. These results are meaningful in two ways. First, JN used a graph-based dependency parsing algorithm that gave higher parsing accuracy for these test sets than the transition-based dependency parsing algorithm used in ClearParser (about 0.9% better in labeled attachment score). Even with poorer parse output, our SRL system performed as well as theirs. Furthermore, our system used only one set of features, which makes the feature engineering easier than JN's approach that used different sets of features for argument identification and classification.

6 Conclusion and future work

This paper makes two contributions. First, we introduce a transition-based semantic role labeling algorithm that shows comparable performance against another state-of-the-art system. The new algorithm takes advantage of using previous predictions as features to make the next predictions. Second, we suggest a self-learning clustering technique that improves labeling accuracy slightly in both the domains. The clustering technique shows potential for improving performance in other new domains.

These preliminary results are promising; however, there is still much room for improvement. Since our algorithm is transition-based, many existing techniques such as k-best ranking (Zhang and Clark, 2008) or dynamic programming (Huang and Sagae, 2010) designed to improve transition-based parsing can be applied. We can also apply different kinds of clustering algorithms to improve the quality of the verb clusters. Furthermore, more features, such as named entity tags or dependency labels, can be used to form a better representation of feature vectors for the clustering.

One of the strongest motivations for designing our transition-based SRL system is to develop a joint-inference system between dependency parsing and semantic role labeling. Since we have already developed a dependency parser, ClearParser, based on a parallel transition-based approach, it will be straightforward to integrate this SRL system with the parser. We will also explore the possiblity of adding empty categories during semantic role labeling.

7 Related work

Nivre (2008) introduced several transition-based dependency parsing algorithms that have been widely used. Johansson and Nugues (2008) and Zhao et al. (2009) presented dependency-based semantic role labelers showing state-of-the-art performance for the CoNLL'08 and '09 shared tasks in English. Scheible (2010) clustered predicate argument structures using EM training and the MDL principle. Wagner et al. (2009) used predicate argument clustering to improve verb sense disambiguation.

Acknowledgments

We gratefully acknowledge the support of the National Science Foundation Grants CISE-IIS-RI-0910992, Richer Representations for Machine Translation, a subcontract from the Mayo Clinic and Harvard Children's Hospital based on a grant from the ONC, 90TR0002/01, Strategic Health Advanced Research Project Area 4: Natural Language Processing, and a grant from the Defense Advanced Research Projects Agency (DARPA/IPTO) under the GALE program, DARPA/CMO Contract No. HR0011-06-C-0022, subcontract from BBN, Inc. Any opinions, findings, and conclusions or recommendations expressed in this material are those of the authors and do not necessarily reflect the views of the National Science Foundation.

References

X. Carreras and L. Màrquez. 2005. Introduction to the conll-2005 shared task: semantic role labeling. In *Proceedings of the Ninth Conference on Computational Natural Language Learning*.

J. D. Choi and M. Palmer. 2010. Retrieving correct semantic boundaries in dependency structure. In *Proceedings of ACL workshop on Linguistic Annotation*.

J. D. Choi and M. Palmer. 2011. Getting the most out of transition-based dependency parsing. In *Proceedings of the 49th Annual Meeting of the Association for Computational Linguistics: Human Language Technologies*.

D. Gildea and D. Jurafsky. 2002. Automatic labeling of semantic roles. *Computational Linguistics*, 28(3).

J. Hajič, M. Ciaramita, R. Johansson, D. Kawahara, M. A. Martí, L. Màrquez, A. Meyers, J. Nivre, S. Padó, J. Štěpánek, P. Straňák, M. Surdeanu, N. Xue, and Y. Zhang. 2009. The conll-2009 shared task: Syntactic and semantic dependencies in multiple languages. In *Proceedings of the 13th Conference on Computational Natural Language Learning: Shared Task*.

J. A. Hartigan. 1975. *Clustering Algorithms*. New York: John Wiley & Sons.

J. Henderson, P. Merlo, G. Musillo, and I. Titov. 2008. A latent variable model of synchronous parsing for syntactic and semantic dependencies. In *Proceedings of the Twelfth Conference on Computational Natural Language Learning*.

T. Hofmann and J. Puzicha. 1998. Statistical models for co-occurrence data. Technical report, Massachusetts Institute of Technology.

C. Hsieh, K. Chang, C. Lin, S. S. Keerthi, and S. Sundararajan. 2008. A dual coordinate descent method for large-scale linear svm. In *Proceedings of the 25th international conference on Machine learning*.

L. Huang and K. Sagae. 2010. Dynamic programming for linear-time incremental parsing. In *Proceedings of the 48th Annual Meeting of the Association for Computational Linguistics*.

R. Johansson and P. Nugues. 2008. Dependency-based semantic role labeling of PropBank. In *Proceedings of the 2008 Conference on Empirical Methods in Natural Language Processing*.

S. D. Kamvar, D. Klein, and C. D. Manning. 2002. Interpreting and extending classical agglomerative clustering algorithms using a model-based approach. In *Proceedings of the 9th International Conference on Machine Learning*.

D. Liu and D. Gildea. 2010. Semantic role features for machine translation. In *Proceedings of the 23rd International Conference on Computational Linguistics*.

C. Lo, J. Luo, and M. Shieh. 2009. Hardware/software codesign of resource constrained real-time systems. In *Proceedings of the 5th International Conference on Information Assurance and Security*.

R. Mcdonald and F. Pereira. 2006. Online learning of approximate dependency parsing algorithms. In *Proceedings of the Annual Meeting of the European American Chapter of the Association for Computational Linguistics*.

J. Nivre. 2008. Algorithms for deterministic incremental dependency parsing. *Computational Linguistics*, 34(4).

M. Palmer, D. Gildea, and P. Kingsbury. 2005. The proposition bank: An annotated corpus of semantic roles. *Computational Linguistics*, 31(1).

S. Pradhan, W. Ward, and J. H. Martin. 2008. Towards robust semantic role labeling. *Computational Linguistics: Special Issue on Semantic Role Labeling*, 34(2).

C. Scheible. 2010. An evaluation of predicate argument clustering using pseudo-disambiguation. In *Proceedings of the 7th conference on International Language Resources and Evaluation*.

D. Shen and M. Lapata. 2007. Using semantic roles to improve question answering. In *Proceedings of the Conference on Empirical Methods in Natural Language Processing and on Computational Natural Language Learning*.

I. Titov, J. Henderson, P. Merlo, and G. Musillo. 2009. Online graph planarisation for synchronous parsing of semantic and syntactic dependencies. In *Proceedings of the 21st International Joint Conference on Artificial Intelligence*.

W. Wagner, H. Schmid, and S. Schulte im Walde. 2009. Verb sense disambiguation using a predicate-argument-clustering model. In *Proceedings of the CogSci Workshop on Distributional Semantics beyond Concrete Concepts*.

J. H. Ward. 1963. Hierarchical grouping to optimize an objective function. *Journal of the American Statistical Association*, 58(301).

N. Xue and M. Palmer. 2004. Calibrating features for semantic role labeling. In *Proceedings of the Conference on Empirical Methods in Natural Language Processing*.

Y. Zhang and S. Clark. 2008. A tale of two parsers: investigating and combining graph-based and transition-based dependency parsing using beam-search. In *Proceedings of the Conference on Empirical Methods in Natural Language Processing*.

H. Zhao, W. Chen, and C. Kit. 2009. Semantic dependency parsing of NomBank and PropBank: An efficient integrated approach via a large-scale feature selection. In *Proceedings of the Conference on Empirical Methods in Natural Language Processing*.

Using Grammar Rule Clusters for Semantic Relation Classification

Emily Jamison
Independent Scholar
Los Alamos, NM 87544, USA
jamison@ling.ohio-state.edu

Abstract

Automatically-derived grammars, such as the split-and-merge model, have proven helpful in parsing (Petrov et al., 2006). As such grammars are refined, latent information is recovered which may be usable for linguistic tasks besides parsing. In this paper, we present and examine a new method of semantic relation classification: using automatically-derived grammar rule clusters as a robust knowledge source for semantic relation classification. We examine performance of this feature group on the SemEval 2010 Relation Classification corpus, and find that it improves performance over both more coarse-grained and more fine-grained syntactic and collocational features in semantic relation classification.

1 Introduction

In the process of discovering a refined grammar starting from rules in the original treebank grammar, latent-variable grammars recover latent information. Intuitively, the new split grammar states should reflect linguistic information that has been generalized from the lexical level but is not so general as the original syntactic level. While the intended use of this information is to improve syntactic parsing, the lexically-derived nature of the split grammar states suggests it may contain semantic information as well.

Petrov et al. (2006) note that while some of these split grammar states reflect true linguistic information, such as the clustering of verbs with similar dependencies, other grammar states may reflect useless information, such as a split between rules that each terminate in a comma. However, it is the automatic nature of grammar splitting which shows potential for deriving semantic knowledge; such split grammar states may reflect statistical and linguistic observations not noticed by humans.

In this paper, we use this recovered latent information for the classification of semantic relations. Our goal is to determine whether recovered latent grammatical information is capable of contributing to the real-world linguistic task of relation classification. We will compare the feature performance of recovered latent information with that of other syntactic and collocational features to determine whether or not the recovered latent information is helpful in semantic relation classification.

2 Task Description

We performed the task of classifying semantic relations from SemEval 2010 Task 8: Multi-way Classification of Semantic Relations between Pairs of Nominals. Each instance consists of a sentence, marked with two nominals, `e1` and `e2`. One of 19 possible direction-sensitive relations is annotated for each pair of nominals. Two examples are shown below.

- The <e1>author</e1> of a keygen uses a <e2>disassembler</e2> to look at the raw assembly code.
  Relation: **Instrument-Agency(e2,e1)**
- Their <e1>knowledge</e1> of the power and rank symbols of the Continental em-

pires was gained from the numerous Germanic <e2>recruits</e2> in the Roman army, and from the Roman practice of enfeoffing various Germanic warrior groups with land in the imperial provinces.
Relation: **Entity-Origin(e1,e2)**

We classified the semantic relations using a Maximum Entropy classifier. In our system, classification was 19-way, direction-sensitive[1] between the classifications: Entity-Origin, Entity-Destination, Cause-Effect, Product-Producer, Content-Container, Instrument-Agency, Member-Collection, Component-Whole, Message-Topic, and Other (non-directional). The model was trained on the 8000-instance training section of the SemEval 2010 Task 8 Semantic Relations Corpus. Distribution of the training data is shown in Table 1 (Hendrickx et al., 2010).

Class	**count**	**% of Data**
Other	1410	17.63%
Cause-Effect	1003	12.54%
Component-Whole	941	11.76%
Entity-Destination	845	10.56%
Product-Producer	717	8.96%
Entity-Origin	716	8.95%
Member-Collection	690	8.63%
Message-Topic	634	7.92%
Content-Container	540	6.75%
Instrument-Agency	504	6.30%

Table 1: Class distribution in the training section of SemEval 2010 Task 8 Semantic Relations Corpus.

We tested the model on the 2717-instance testing section of the same corpus. For each instance, the user was provided with a sentence containing two marked entities, `e1` and `e2`. We structured the task such that, for each instance, we chose the best semantic relation out of the 19 available.

In this paper, we use grammatical cluster information (i.e., recovered latent information) from the Berkeley Parser (Petrov 2006) as semantic features of syntactic origin to classify semantic relations in the SemEval 2010 Semantic Relations corpus, in a Maximum Entropy model. We conduct two sets of experiments. In the first experiment, we examine the effect of using Berkeley Parser latent cluster features to enhance specificity over more general features (POS tags and others), where the cluster features are inherently more closely tuned with the data than the other features, and more likely to lead to an overfitted model. In the second experiment, we examine the effect of using cluster features to enhance generalizability over more specific features (the words of the cluster features' terminal nodes), in which case the cluster features generalize over othe more specific features, but are more likely to miss detailed patterns.

[1]i.e., with a Content-Container relation, the nominal that is the container and the nominal that is the content cannot be reversed.

2.1 Previous Work

The classification of semantic relations has been proposed to help NLP tasks ranging from word sense disambiguation, language modelling, paraphrasing, and recognising textual entailment (Hendrickx et al., 2010).

Semantic world knowledge is crucial for accurate semantic classification of many types, and sources range from the hand-crafted-yet sparse (such as WordNet) to the robust-yet-noisy (such as the Internet). For this community task, teams proposed a variety of knowledge sources and other features for their relation classification, from knowledge databases (Tymoshenko and Giuliano, 2010), WordNet (Rink and Harabagiu, 2010), Wikipedia (Szarvas and Gurevych, 2010), to formal linguistic Levin classes (Rink and Harabagiu, 2010), to collocational metrics (Rink and Harabagiu, 2010) and stems (Chen et al., 2010).

Syntactic features present special benefits to any semantic classification task: they can generalize over the local context in ways that collocational metrics cannot, and unlike knowledge database sources which assign the most common word sense to a word, syntactic features are sensitive to the word's sense, as determined by the local context of the word. Several teams in SemEval 2010 Task 8 used syntactic features for semantic relation classification. Chen et al. (2010) use a feature set of the syntactic parent node held in common by the two nominals. Rink and Harabagiu (2010) use a feature set of dependency paths of length 1 or 2 from the dependency tree around the two nominals.

2.2 Grammatical cluster information

For our investigations, we used the Berkeley Parser (Petrov et al 2006, Petrov and Klein 2007) as a source of grammar rule clusters. We used the eng_sm6.gr off-the-shelf model.

The Berkeley Parser starts with an initial grammar extracted from Wall Street Journal corpus sections 2-22. The parser then tries to learn a set of rule probabilities over latent annotations to maximize the likelihood of the training trees using Expectation-Maximization (EM).

Consider a sentence w and its unannotated tree T, a non-terminal A spanning (r, t), and its children B and C spanning (r, s) and (s, t). A_x is a subsymbol of A, B_x of B, and C_x of C. We calculate the posterior probability of all annotated rules and positions for each training set tree T in the Expectation step (Petrov et al., 2006):

$$P((r,s,t,A_x \rightarrow B_y C_z) \mid w, T) \propto \mathbf{P}_{\text{OUT}}(r,t,A_x) \times \beta(A_x \rightarrow B_y C_z) \mathbf{P}_{\text{IN}}(r,s,B_y) \mathbf{P}_{\text{IN}}(s,t,C_z) \quad (1)$$

The probabilities from the Expectation step act as weighted observations to update the rule probabilities in the Maximization step:

$$\beta(A_x \rightarrow B_y C_z) := \frac{\#\{A_x \rightarrow B_y C_z\}}{\Sigma_{y',z'} \#\{A_x \rightarrow B_{y'} C_{z'}\}} \quad (2)$$

In each cycle of EM, the grammar is split randomly in halves, and some halves are merged back together. The grammar is retrained, and the results are used to initialize the next round of EM.

In the splitting step, all grammatical nodes are split in two. Although the grammar grows more finely fitted to the training data with each splitting step, its size quickly becomes unmanageable, its rules become overfitted, and because the splits are not a result of likelihood calculation, many unhelpful rules are produced. The merging step functions to remove unhelpful rules. In the merging step, each split is examined for the loss of likelihood removing it would cause; splits whose likelihood contribution is below a cutoff are re-combined.

The experiments we perform in this paper are a gamble on the possibility that the saved splits are picking up semantic information from the rule structure they reflect in the increased likelihood. We use the final split cluster ID's (PP-5, PP-8, etc.) as features in our experiments.[2]

2.3 Features

We used several sets of features in our experiments. All POS-tags, syntactic structure, and Cluster ID features come from the Berkeley Parser. The lemmatization comes from Morpha (Minnen et al., 2001). All features occurring less than two times in the training data were discarded, for ease of processing. A sample sentence and the resulting features are shown in Table 2. Note that all features, collocational and syntactic, were used for discovering semantic knowledge.

	The Crayola <e1>*box*</e1> *contained two* <e2>*pencils*</e2>.
SW	the-dt, crayola-jj, contain-vbd, two-cd, pencil-nns, box-nn
IBW	contained, two, contained∧two
OCW	crayola-jj, box-nn, contain-vbd, pencil-nns
POS-tags	vbd, cd, vbd∧cd
ID's	vbd6, cd1, vbd6∧cd1

Table 2: A sample sentence and its accompanying features.

Collocational Features:

- **Surrounding Words (SW):** From Ye and Baldwin's (2007) preposition sense disambiguation system, this set of features consists of lemmas of all of the words within a window of seven words before and after each of **e1** and **e2**. Features are not, however, marked with relative location, as we found that this reduced accuracy.

- **In-Between Words (IBW):** This bag of features consists of the string of words occuring in the sentence in between **e1** and **e2**, exclusive, as well as all the substrings of those consecutive words. We tried marking each feature with its relative location, but we found that results improved without location marking, and so we do not use location marking in these experiments.

[2]Note that cluster ID's are only meaningful when compared to other cluster ID's split from the same parent node.

Syntactic Features:

- **Open Class Words (OCW):** from Ye and Baldwin's (2007) preposition sense disambiguation system, this set of features consists of the lemmas of all of the open-class words in the sentence (i.e., NP, VP, ADJP, ADVP).

- **POS-tags:** The POS tags of the words (i.e., terminal nodes) and all consecutive strings of POS tags in between **e1** and **e2**, exclusive. Tags are from the Berkeley Parser.

- **Cluster ID's:** The Berkeley Parser syntactic rule cluster ID's and POS-tags of the terminal nodes in between **e1** and **e2**. ID numbers are only relevant when comparing ID's with the same POS tag.

3 Experiment: Cluster ID's as more spcific features

In our first experiment, we compared two systems of Surrounding Words, Open-Class Words, and In-Between Terminal Tags, with and without In-Between Terminal Cluster ID's. The results are shown in Table 3.

3.1 Results and Analysis

Table 3 shows the results of adding more specific Cluster ID features to the more general POS-tag, Open-Class, and Surrounding-Words features. While this could have led to an over-fitted model, apparently it did not. Overall precision increased from 66.60% to 68.62%, an increase of 2.02%, yet recall also increased, from 64.26% to 65.33%, an increase of 1.07%. The more precise, more closely-fitted features did not harm performance, but actually enhanced it. The Maximum Entropy learner itself preferred the Cluster ID features: Table 4 shows per-class POS-tag and Cluster-ID features with a lambda value over 0.25, comparing when both POS-tag features and Cluster ID tags are available, versus just POS-tags (all among other features used in Experiment 1). When given the opportunity, the MaxEnt learner considered the Cluster ID features more important than the POS-tag features.

As shown in Table 3, we can see that adding the Cluster ID's did mildly increase F-measure (by 1.41 %, from 65.01% to 66.42%[3]. However, when viewed on a class-by-class basis, some classes show great improvement with the addition of Cluster ID's while others remain unchanged. The classes *Cause-Effect*, *Component-Whole*, *Content-Container*, *Instrument-Agency*, and *Message-Topic* all gained significantly with the addition of cluster ID features. We investigated important features of these classes more carefully.

Classes that significantly improved with Cluster ID's:

- **Cause-Effect**: Cluster ID features that correlated highly with **Cause-Effect**, besides keyword-type single word clusters (*from*, *that*), were a cluster of certain occurances of the prepositions *by*, *from*, *of*, *in*; and a cluster of cause-type verbs (shown in Table 5) plus the phrase *by*.
- **Content-Container**: Features positively correlated with **Content-Container**, besides some keywords and phrases such as *full of*, *was*, *in*, and *the/a*, included a Cluster ID feature with a number of verbs commonly used to refer to containers and the processes of filling and emptying them, such as *leaked*, *contained*, *poured*, *stuffed*, *took*, *injected*, *inserted*, and *found*. The verbs from this feature are listed in Table 6.
- **Instrument-Agency**: Several Cluster ID features of verbs correlate with this class. Although it is not as obvious as the verb list with **Cause-Effect**, Table 7 compares several verb clusters that did have a noticeable positive correlation with **Instrument-Agency** with several verb clusters of the same POS-tags that did not correlate.
- **Component-Whole**: Notable keyword and key phrase features include *of the/a/an*, *has a*, and *has*. One Cluster ID feature is a cluster of third-person, possessive, and reflexive pronouns. Al-

[3]An F-measure of 66.42% would have put our system in the middle of the pack on Task performance if it had participated in the actual SemEval 2010 Task 8. Task results for the entire dataset ranged from 82.18% F-m with a carefully-design knowledge database, to 52.16% with parse features, NE's, and semantic seed lists, and 26.67% using punctuation, prepositional patterns, and context words. Our goal, however, is to determine whether recovered latent grammatical information is capable of contributing to relation classification at all.

	Precision			Recall			F-measure		
Class	**no ID**	**w/ ID**	**diff**	**no ID**	**w/ ID**	**diff**	**no ID**	**w/ ID**	**diff**
Cause-Effect	79.43	82.62	**3.19**	76.52	76.83	0.31	77.95	79.62	**1.67**
Component-Whole	56.58	61.86	**5.28**	55.13	57.69	**2.56**	55.84	59.70	**3.86**
Content-Container	74.37	77.04	**2.67**	77.08	78.65	1.57	75.70	77.84	**2.14**
Entity-Destination	73.30	72.60	-0.70	88.36	88.01	-0.35	80.12	79.57	-0.55
Entity-Origin	67.42	66.67	-0.75	69.77	69.77	0.00	68.57	68.18	-0.35
Instrument-Agency	55.73	56.30	0.57	46.79	48.72	1.93	50.87	52.23	**1.36**
Member-Collection	68.40	67.57	-0.83	73.39	75.11	1.72	70.81	71.14	0.33
Message-Topic	65.95	70.47	**4.52**	46.74	52.11	**5.37**	54.71	59.91	**5.20**
Product-Producer	58.19	62.50	**4.31**	44.59	41.13	-3.46	50.49	49.61	-0.88
Other	30.97	28.65	**-2.32**	36.56	35.46	-1.10	33.54	31.69	-1.85
Total, Macro-Avg	66.60	68.62	2.02	64.26	65.33	1.07	65.01	66.42	1.41

Table 3: Comparison of Open-Class Words, Surrounding Words, and POS-tags, with and without Cluster ID features. Per SemEval2010 task standards, total does not include 'Other'. Directionality is evaluated, but results are combined for viewability. Bold-font differences are most notable.

	POS only	**POS & Cluster ID**	
Class	**POS**	**POS**	**ID's**
Cause-Effect	5	0	6
Component-Whole	4	1	6
Content-Container	4	0	7
Entity-Destination	4	0	4
Entity-Origin	2	1	6
Instrument-Agency	7	0	6
Member-Collection	3	0	2
Message-Topic	3	0	6
Product-Producer	5	1	5
Other	1	1	0

Table 4: Number of POS-tag and Cluster ID features with a lambda value over 0.25, with and without Cluster ID features being available. High lambda values are assigned when a classifier finds the features has a high positive correlation with correct examples in the training data.

though it is a somewhat rare feature, when it occurs it is positively-correlated. An example of a **Component-Whole** pronoun is below:

> He stopped rowing when the boat was opposite to the paddle wheel of the steamer, and the <e1>steamer</e1> stopped **her** <e2>engine</e2> at the same time.

accompanied, affected, built, caused, completed, composed, contained, cooked, covered, created, derived, developed, discovered, distilled, driven, enclosed, fabricated, followed, founded, generated, given, known, led, made, manufactured, obtained, offered, produced, published, raised, represented, run, shared, supported, transmitted, triggered, used, wrapped, written

Table 5: Contents of the VBN-12 Cluster that occurred 3 or more times in the Relational Semantics corpus training data. Many of the verbs denote a cause-effect relationship.

- **Message-Topic**: Some helpful keyword features were *in*, *to*, and *that*. A helpful Cluster ID feature was a cluster of the prepositions *about*, *over*, *upon*, *around*, and *between*. The model also ranked highly a Cluster ID feature containing a number of 'discussion' and 'document' verbs, shown in Table 8.

Classes that did not significantly improve with Cluster ID's:

- **Entity-Origin**: This class is suspected to have been plagued by faulty annotation. 7 out of the first 24 training examples are incorrectly marked as **Entity-Origin**, according to the corpus's definitions. This noise in the data likely prevents effective comparison of features. Despite the noise, some clusters with a high correlation to the class include: a cluster of verbs

adjusted, applied, became, brought, built, caused, contained, created, described, did, established, examined, featured, followed, formed, found, gave, included, injected, inserted, introduced, involved, joined, leaked, made, marked, posted, poured, produced, released, reported, saw, sent, spotted, stuffed, took, used, was, were, won, wrote, wrapped, written

Table 6: Contents of the VBD-5 Cluster that occurred 3 or more times in the Relational Semantics corpus training data. A number of the verbs can refer to actions involving containers and their contents.

consisting of mostly *made*, *kept*, and *left*; and a cluster of verbs consisting mostly of *made*, *left*, *kept*, *departed*, *arrived*, *travelled*, and *consisted*.

- **Entity-Destination**: The Cluster ID features that correlated highly with this class mark individual key words and phrases: *for the*, *on the*, *to the*, and *to*. Clusters of words were not helpful for this class.

- **Product-Producer**: The Cluster ID features that strongly correlated with this class consisted mostly of the words *who/whom* and *by*; individual key word features would have been just as good. Several clusters of verbs were highly correlated as well, but apparently there was too much noise in the clusters for them to be effective.

- **Member-Collection**: This class used the 'jj-24' POS cluster, which contains the word *other* among other adjectives. This is probably from the classic **Member-Collection** phrase "Y and other X's". However, this features, along with a feature mostly consisting of *of*, was not enough to make much difference (0.33%) over POS features.

- **Other**: The class *Other* decreased in F-measure with the addition of cluster ID features. Combined with the overall F-measure increase for all the regular classes, we interpret this decrease in F-measure as an increase in entropy, as more examples with identifiable useful features are removed from the *Other* category, and the MaxEnt learner has fewer accurate patterns with which to cluster this diverse group of examples. In order words, we actually desire to see a decrease in *Other* F-measure, as the examples in *Other* have almost nothing in common with eachother and should be hard to identify.

Overall, some of the semantic relation classes were correlated with features of syntactic clusters, and the clusters boosted scores, while other classes weren't, and their scores remained roughly the same. The results of this experiment show that syntactic clusters did not lead to overtraining of data, and were helpful with semantic relation classification.

4 Experiment: Cluster ID's as more general features

In our second experiment, using the same experimental set-up but different features, we compared In-Between Words (IBW), IBW Plus POS-tags, and IBW Plus POS-tags Plus Cluster ID features. The results are shown in Table 9. The goal of this experiment is to compare Cluster ID features to an even more fine-grained feature, the words themselves. The words, POS-tags, and Cluster ID tags all concern the same nodes in the sentence.

4.1 Results and Analysis

Table 9 shows the results of adding coarser-grained Cluster ID features to the more specific In-Between-Words features, as well as to the POS-tag features. The addition of Cluster ID features improved classification over IBW plus POS-tags, as well as IBW alone. While the previous experiment showed that Cluster ID features were not too specific to be helpful, this experiment shows that they are also not too general as to blur lexical patterns. While overall F-measure increased 2.13% from IBW with the addition of POS-tag features, from 63.35% to 65.48%, F-measure also increased further by the addition of Cluster ID features to IBW plus POS-tags, with a total increase of 2.72% over IBW features alone, from 63.35% to 66.07%.

Table 10 breaks down results into Precision and Recall for the different groups of features. Since this experiment was starting with a more precise base-

Cluster	Words
	Instrument-Agency Positively-correlated Clusters:
VBD-7	approached, arrived, attached, bought, built, carried, caught, changed, chose, clicked, contained, covered, deposited, described, directed, donated, dragged, dropped, entered, erected, established, explained, fetched, fired, fled, gave, grabbed, hit, inserted, joined, kept, killed, knew, left, lived, lost, made, moved, noticed, observed, opened, organized, packed, passed, performed, placed, poured, prepared, presented, pressed, pulled, pushed, put, removed, rescheduled, saw, scaled, searched, sent, sold, spent, stirred, struck, stuffed, threw, took, tore, turned, used, was, wrote
VBZ-9	applies, assists, brings, builds, changes, comprises, considers, contains, converts, covers, creates, cuts, describes, emits, encloses, enters, gets, hits, holds, joins, keeps, leaves, makes, needs, offers, plays, portrays, prepares, provides, removes, s, spreads, stirs, studies, teaches, uses, writes
	Non-positively-correlated Clusters:
VBD-4	became, bought, carried, caused, completed, contained, created, developed, dug, filled, formed, got, had, held, issued, killed, made, presented, produced, reached, received, required, saw, showed, stopped, took, triggered
VBD-9	began, kept, started, stopped
VBD-8	continued, decided, had, happened, managed, needed, seemed, tried, used, wanted
VBD-2	found, learned, noted, noticed, read, revealed, saw
VBZ-8	arrives, brings, comes, comprises, consists, contains, contributes, copes, departs, extends, falls, feels, flows, focuses, goes, grows, hangs, leads, looks, moves, originates, passes, pulls, refers, relates, rests, results, returns, runs, s, sits, speaks, starts, stops, talks, travels, uprises

Table 7: Some positively-correlating and non-correlating verb clusters for **Instrument-Agency**. Verbs occurred at least 3 times in the Relational Semantics corpus training data. Many verbs from positively-correlating Cluster ID features may occur with mention of a tool or object to be used to carry out the action.

attaches, builds, carries, causes, combines, comprises, contains, creates, describes, discusses, encloses, gives, holds, includes, keeps, makes, manipulates, means, needs, offers, performs, presents, processes, provides, represents, requires, s, shows, takes, wears, writes

Table 8: Contents of the VBZ-11 Cluster that occurred 3 or more times in the Relational Semantics corpus training data. Many of the verbs are associated with documents or speaking.

line, IBW features, and adding coarser grained features, POS-tags and Cluster IDs, we might expect to see a simultaneous decrease in precision and increase in recall from the baseline IBW to the enhanced, POS-tag and Cluster ID versions. As can be seen in Table 10, this is exactly what happens. However, Cluster ID features are found to be helpful to the overall goal of semantic relation classification, because they increase recall by much more (4.44%) than they decrease precision (-0.44%).

Classes for which the Cluster ID plus POS-tag plus IBW combo was highest include **Content-Container**, **Entity-Destination**, **Member-Collection**, **Message-Topic**, and **Other**. **Component-Whole**, **Instrument-Agency**, and **Product-Producer** all showed gains over just IBW, but had lower scores than IBW plus just POS-tags. Only **Cause-Effect** and **Entity-Origin** failed to show any improvement with POS-tags or Cluster ID's over the baseline IBW features.

A comparison of features between Experiments 1 and 2 showed that nearly all of the significantly helpful positive-corellated Cluster ID features (with lambda greater than 0.25) in Experiment 2 were also important in Experiment 1. Some cluster ID features in Experiment 1 that isolated out a single word were replaced in Experiment 2 by a more-accurate individual IBW word feature.

5 Conclusion

In this paper, we presented a new method of semantic relation classification: using automatically-derived grammar rule clusters as a semantic knowledge source for relation classification. We tested performance of the feature on the SemEval 2010 Relation Classification corpus, and found that it improved performance over both more coarse-grained

	F-measure				
Class	**IBW**	**+POS**	**IBW+POS diff**	**+ID**	**IBW+ID diff**
Cause-Effect	**83.39**	80.19	-3.20	81.55	-1.84
Component-Whole	52.50	56.07	**3.57**	55.06	2.56
Content-Container	73.79	73.27	-0.52	75.19	**1.40**
Entity-Destination	77.98	80.06	2.08	81.49	**3.51**
Entity-Origin	**68.56**	67.21	-1.35	67.33	-1.23
Instrument-Agency	54.29	56.43	**2.14**	55.63	1.34
Member-Collection	73.22	75.30	2.08	75.50	**2.28**
Message-Topic	39.59	47.06	7.47	49.45	**9.86**
Product-Producer	46.88	53.77	**6.89**	53.46	6.58
Other	27.69	30.08	2.39	30.63	**2.94**
Total, Macro-Avg	63.35	65.48	2.13	66.07	**2.72**

Table 9: F-measure comparison of In-Between Words, IBW plus POS-tags, and IBW plus POS-tags plus Cluster ID features. Per SemEval2010 task standards, total does not include **Other**. Bold-font differences are the highest improvements (or baseline, whichever is higher).

Analysis	**iBW**	**+POS**	**iBW +POS diff**	**+ID**	**iBW +ID diff**
Precision	**67.03**	66.28	-0.75	66.59	-0.44
Recall	62.10	66.12	4.02	**66.54**	4.44

Table 10: Comparison of IBW, IBW plus POS-tags, and IBW plus POS-tags plus Cluster ID features. Per SemEval2010 Task 8 standards, total does not include **Other**. Bold-font differences are the highest improvements (or baseline).

and more fine-grained syntactic and collocational features in semantic relation classification.

Acknowledgments

The author wishes to thank William Schuler and Yannick Versley for their advice and support on this project.

References

Yuan Chen , Man Lan , Jian Su , Zhi Min Zhou , Yu Xu 2010. ECNU: Effective Semantic Relations Classification without Complicated Features or Multiple External Corpora. *Proceedings of the 5th International Workshop on Semantic Evaluation.*

Iris Hendrickx , Su Nam Kim , Zornitsa Kozareva , Preslav Nakov , Diarmuid O Seaghdha , Sebastian Pado, Marco Pennacchiotti , Lorenza Romano, Stan Szpakowicz. 2010. SemEval-2010 Task 8: Multi-Way Classification of Semantic Relations Between Pairs of Nominals. *Proceedings of the 5th International Workshop on Semantic Evaluation.*

Guido Minnen, John Carroll, and Darren Pearce. 2001. Applied morphological processing of English. *Natural Language Engineering*, 7(3):207223.

Slav Petrov, Leon Barrett, Romain Thibaux, and Dan Klein. 2006. Learning Accurate, Compact, and Interpretable Tree Annotation. In *Proceedings of the 21st International Conference on Computational Linguistics and the 44th Annual Meeting of the Association of Computational Linguistics.*

Slav Petrov and Dan Klein. 2007. Improved Inference for Unlexicalized Parsing. *Proceedings of NAACL 2007.*

Bryan Rink and Sanda Harabagiu 2010. UTD: Classifying Semantic Relations by Combining Lexical and Semantic Resources. *Proceedings of the 5th International Workshop on Semantic Evaluation.*

Gyorgy Szarvas and Iryna Gurevych 2010. TUD: semantic relatedness for relation classification *Proceedings of the 5th International Workshop on Semantic Evaluation.*

Kateryna Tymoshenko and Claudio Giuliano. 2010. FBK-IRST: Semantic Relation Extraction using Cyc. *Proceedings of the 5th International Workshop on Semantic Evaluation.*

Patrick Ye and Timothy Baldwin. 2007. MELB-YB: Preposition Sense Disambiguation Using Rich Semantic Features. *Proceedings of SemEval 2007.*

Desperately Seeking Implicit Arguments in Text

Sara Tonelli
Fondazione Bruno Kessler / Trento, Italy
satonelli@fbk.eu

Rodolfo Delmonte
Universit Ca' Foscari / Venezia, Italy
delmont@unive.it

Abstract

In this paper, we address the issue of automatically identifying null instantiated arguments in text. We refer to Fillmore's theory of pragmatically controlled zero anaphora (Fillmore, 1986), which accounts for the phenomenon of omissible arguments using a *lexically-based* approach, and we propose a strategy for identifying implicit arguments in a text and finding their antecedents, given the overtly expressed semantic roles in the form of frame elements. To this purpose, we primarily rely on linguistic knowledge enriched with role frequency information collected from a training corpus. We evaluate our approach using the test set developed for the SemEval task 10 and we highlight some issues of our approach. Besides, we also point out some open problems related to the task definition and to the general phenomenon of null instantiated arguments, which needs to be better investigated and described in order to be captured from a computational point of view.

1 Introduction

In natural language, lexically unexpressed linguistic items are very frequent and indirectly weaken any attempt at computing the meaning of a text or discourse. However, the need to address semantic interpretation is strongly felt in current advanced NLP tasks, in particular, the issue of transforming a text or discourse into a set of explicitly interconnected predicate-argument/adjunct structures (hence PAS). The aim of this task would be to unambiguously identify events and participants and their association to spatiotemporal locations. However, in order to do that, symbolic and statistical approaches should be based on the output representation of a deep parser, which is currently almost never the case. Current NLP technologies usually address the surface level linguistic information with good approximation in dependency or constituency structures, but miss implicit entities (IEs) altogether. The difficulties to deal with lexically unexpressed items or implicit entities are related on the one hand to recall problems, i.e. the problem of deciding whether an item is implicit or not, and on the other hand to precision problems, i.e. if an implicit entity is accessible to the reader from the discourse or its context, an appropriate antecedent has to be found. However, a system able to derive the presence of IEs may be a determining factor in improving performance of QA systems and, in general, in Informations Retrieval and Extraction systems.

The current computational scene has witnessed an increased interest in the creation and use of semantically annotated computational lexica and their associated annotated corpora, like PropBank (Palmer et al., 2005), FrameNet (Baker et al., 1998) and NomBank (Meyers, 2007), where the proposed annotation scheme has been applied in real contexts. In all these cases, what has been addressed is a basic semantic issue, i.e. labeling PAS associated to semantic predicates like adjectives, verbs and nouns. However, what these corpora have not made available is information related to IEs. For example, in the case of eventive deverbal nominals, information about the subject/object of the nominal predicate is often implicit and has to be understood from the previous discourse or text, e.g. *"the development of a prototype [→ implicit subject]"*. As reported by Gerber and Chai (2010), introducing implicit arguments to nominal predicates in NomBank would increase the resource coverage of 65%.

Other IEs can be found in agentless passive constructions (e.g.*"Our little problem will soon be solved ∅ [→ unexpressed Agent]"*[1]) or as unexpressed arguments such as addressee with verbs of commitment, for example *"I can promise ∅ that one of you will be troubled [→ unexpressed Addressee]"* and *"I dare swear ∅ that before tomorrow night he will be fluttering in our net [→ unexpressed Addressee]"*.

In this paper we discuss the issues related to the identification of implicit entities in text, focussing in particular on omissions of core arguments of predicates. We investigate the topic from the perspective proposed by (Fillmore, 1986) and base our observations on null instantiated arguments annotated for the SemEval 2010 Task 10, 'Linking Events and Their Participants in Discourse' (Ruppenhofer et al., 2010)[2]. The paper is structured as follows: in Section 2 we detail the task of identifying null instantiated arguments from a theoretical perspective and describe related work. In Section 3 we briefly introduce the SemEval task 10 for identifying implicit arguments in text, while in Section 4 we detail our proposal for NI identification and binding. In Section 5 we give a thorough description of the types of null instantiations annotated in the SemEval data set and we explain the behavior of our algorithm w.r.t. such cases. We also compare our results with the output of the systems participating to the SemEval task. Finally, we draw some conclusions in Section 6.

2 Related work

In this work, we focus on *null complements*, also called pragmatically controlled zero anaphora (Fillmore, 1986), understood arguments or linguistically unrealized arguments. We focus on Fillmore's theory because his approach represents the backbone of the FrameNet project, which in turn inspired the SemEval task we will describe below. Fillmore (1986) shows that in English and many other languages some verbs allow null complements and some others don't. The latter require that, when they appear in a sentence, all core semantic roles related to the predicate are expressed. For example, sentences like *"Mary locked* **" or *"John guaranteed* **" are not grammatically well-formed, because they both require two mandatory linguistically inherent participants. Fillmore tries to explain why semantic roles can sometimes be left unspoken and what constraints help the interpreter recover the missing roles. He introduces different factors that can influence the licensing of null complements. These can be *lexically-based*, (semantically close predicates like 'promise' and 'guarantee' can license the omission of the theme argument in different cases), motivated by the *interpretation of the predicate* (*"I was eating ∅"* licenses a null object because it has an existential interpretation) and depending on the context (see for example the use of *impress* in an episodic context like *"She impressed the audience"*, where the null complement is not allowed, compared to *"She impresses ∅ every time"* in habitual interpretation; examples from Ruppenhofer and Michaelis (2009)).

The fact that Fillmore explains the phenomenon of omissible arguments with a lexically-based approach implies that from his perspective neither a purely pragmatic nor a purely semantic approach can account for the behavior of omissible arguments. For example, he argues that some verbs, such as *to lock* will never license a null complement, no matter in which pragmatic context they are used. Besides, there are synonymous verbs which behave differently as regards null complementation, which Fillmore sees as evidence against a purely semantic explanation of implicit arguments.

Another relevant distinction drawn in Fillmore (1986) is the typology of omitted arguments, which depends on the type of licensor and on the interpretation of the null complement. Fillmore claims that with some verbs the missing complement can be retrieved from the context, i.e. it is possible to find a referent previously mentioned in the text / discourse

[1] Unless otherwise specified, the following examples are taken from the data sets made available in the SemEval 2010 task 'Linking Events and Their Participants in Discourse'. Some of them have been slightly simplified for purposes of exposition.

[2] http://semeval2.fbk.eu/semeval2.php?location=tasks&taskid=9

and bearing a definite, precise meaning. These cases are labeled as *definite null complements* or *instantiations* (DNI) and are *lexically specific* in that they apply only to some predicates. We report an example of DNI in (1), taken from the SemEval task 10 data set (see Section 3). The predicate '*waiting*' has an omitted object, which we understand from the discourse context to refer to '*I*'.

(1) I saw him rejoin his guest, and *I* crept quietly back to where my companions were *waiting* ∅ to tell them what I had seen.

DNIs can also occur with nominal predicates, as reported in (2), where the person having a *thought*, *the baronet*, is mentioned in the preceding sentence:

(2) Stapleton was talking with animation, but *the baronet* looked pale and distrait. Perhaps the *thought* of that lonely walk across the ill-omened moor was weighing heavily upon his mind.

In contrast to DNIs, Fillmore claims that with some verbs and in some interpretations, a core argument can be omitted without having a referent expressing the meaning of the null argument. The identity of the missing argument can be left unknown or indefinite. These cases are labeled as *indefinite null complements* or *instantiations* (INI) and are *constructionally licensed* in that they apply to any predicate in a particular grammatical construction. See for example the following cases, where the omission of the agent is licensed by the passive construction:

(3) One of them was suddenly *shut off* ∅.

(4) I am *reckoned* fleet of foot ∅.

Cases of INI were annotated by the organizers of the SemEval task 10 also with nominal predicates, as shown in the example below, where the perceiver of the *odour* is left unspecified:

(5) Rank reeds and lush, slimy water-plants sent an *odour* ∅ of decay and a heavy miasmatic vapour.

Few attempts have been done so far to automatically deal with the recovery of implicit information in text. One of the earliest systems for identifying extra-sentential arguments is PUNDIT by Palmer et al. (1986). This Prolog-based system comprises a syntactic component for parsing, a semantic component, which decomposes predicates into component meanings and fills their semantic roles with syntactic constituents based on a domain-specific model, and a reference resolution component, which is called both for explicit constituents and for obligatory implicit constituents. The reference resolution process is based on a focus list with all potential pronominal referents identified by the semantic component. The approach, however, has not been evaluated on a data set, so we cannot directly compare its performance with other approaches. Furthermore, it is strongly domain-dependent.

In a case study, Burchardt et al. (2005) propose to identify implicit arguments exploiting contextual relations from deep-parsing and lexico-semantic frame relations encoded in FrameNet. In particular, they suggest converting a text into a network of lexico-semantic predicate-argument relations connected through frame-to-frame relations and recurrent anaphoric linking patterns. However, the authors do not implement and evaluate this approach.

Most recently, Gerber and Chai (2010) have presented a supervised classification model for the recovery of implicit arguments of nominal predicates in NomBank. The model features are quite different from those usually considered in standard SRL tasks and include among others information from VerbNet classes, pointwise mutual information between semantic arguments, collocation and frequency information about the predicates, information about parent nodes and siblings of the predicates and discourse information. The authors show the feasibility of their approach, which however relies on a selected group of nominal predicates with a large number of annotated instances.

The first attempt to evaluate implicit argument identification over a common test set and considering different kinds of predicates was made by Ruppenhofer et al. (2010). Further details are given in the following section.

Data set	Sentences	Frame inst.	Frame types	Overt FEs	DNIs (resolved)	INIs
Train	438	1,370	317	2,526	303 (245)	277
Test	525	1,703	452	3,141	349 (259)	361

Table 1: Data set statistics from SemEval task 10

3 SemEval 2010 task 10

The SemEval-2010 task for linking events and their participants in discourse (Ruppenhofer et al., 2010) introduced a new issue w.r.t. the SemEval-2007 task 'Frame Semantic Structure Extraction' (Baker et al., 2007), in that it focused on linking local semantic argument structures across sentence boundaries. Specifically, the task included first the identification of frames and frame elements in a text following the FrameNet paradigm (Baker et al., 1998), then the identification of locally uninstantiated roles (NIs). If these roles are indefinite (INI), they have to be marked as such and no antecedent has to be found. On the contrary, if they are definite (DNI), their coreferents have to be found in the wider discourse context. The challenge comprised two tasks, namely the full task (semantic role recognition and labeling + NI linking) and the NIs only task, i.e. the identification of null instantiations and their referents given a test set with gold standard local semantic argument structure. In this work, we focus on the latter task.

The data provided to the participants included a training and a test set. The training data comprised 438 sentences from Arthur Conan Doyle's novel 'The Adventure of Wisteria Lodge', manually annotated with frame and INI/DNI information. The test set included 2 chapters of the Sherlock Holmes story 'The Hound of Baskervilles' with a total of 525 sentences, provided with gold standard frame information. The participants had to *i)* assess if a local argument is implicit; *ii)* decide whether it is an INI or a DNI and *iii)* in the second case, find the antecedent of the implicit argument. We report in Table 1 some statistics about the provided data sets from Ruppenhofer et al. (2010). Note that overt FEs are the explicit frame elements annotated in the data set.

Although 26 teams downloaded the data sets, there were only two submissions, probably depending on the intrinsic difficulties of the task (see discussion in Section 5). The best performing system (Chen et al., 2010) is based on a supervised learning approach using, among others, distributional semantic similarity between the heads of candidate referents and role fillers in the training data, but its performance is strongly affected by data sparseness. Indeed, only 438 sentences with annotated NIs were made available in the training set, which is clearly insufficient to capture such a multifaceted phenomenon with a supervised approach. The second system participating in the task (Tonelli and Delmonte, 2010) was an adaptation of an existing LFG-based system for deep semantic analysis (Delmonte, 2009), whose output was mapped to FrameNet-style annotation. In this case, the major challenge was to cope with the classification of some NI phenomena which are very much dependent on frame specific information, and can hardly be generalized in the LFG framework.

4 A linguistically motivated proposal for NI identification and binding

In this section, we describe our proposal for dealing with INI/DNI identification and evaluate our output against SemEval gold standard data. As discussed in the previous section, existing systems dealing with this task suffer on the one hand from a lack of training data and on the other hand from the dependence of the task on frame annotation, which makes it difficult to adapt existing unsupervised approaches. We show that, given this state of the art, better results can be achieved in the task by simply developing an algorithm that reflects as much as possible the linguistic motivations behind NI identification in the FrameNet paradigm. Our approach is divided into two subtasks: *i)* identify INIs/DNIs and *ii)* for each DNI, find the corresponding referent in text.

We develop an algorithm that incorporates the following linguistic information:

FE coreness status Null instantiated arguments as defined in FrameNet are always *core* arguments, i.e.

they are central to the meaning of a frame. Since the coreness status of the arguments is encoded in FrameNet, we limit our search for an NI only if a core frame element is not overtly expressed in the text.

Incorporated FEs Although all lexical units belonging to the same frame in the FrameNet database are characterized by the same set of core FEs, a further distinction should be introduced when dealing with NIs identification. For example, in PERCEPTION_ACTIVE, several predicates are listed, which however have a different behavior w.r.t. the core *Body_part* FE. 'Feel.v', for instance, is underspecified as regards the body part perceiving the sensation, so we can assume that when it is not overtly expressed, we have a case of null instantiation. For other verbs in the same frame, such as 'glance.v' or 'listen.v', the coreness status of *Body_part* seems to be more questionable, because the perceiving organ is already implied by the verb meaning. For this reason, we argue that if *Body_part* is not expressed with 'glance.v' or 'listen.v', it is not a case of null instantiation. Such FEs are defined as *incorporated* in the lexical unit and are encoded as such in FrameNet.

Excludes and Includes relation In FrameNet, some information about the relationship between certain FEs is encoded. In particular, some FEs are connected by the *Excludes* relation, which means that they cannot occur together, and others by the *Requires* relation, which means that if a given FE is present, then also the other must be overtly or implicitly present. An example of *Excludes* is the relationship between the FE *Entity_1 / Entity_2* and *Entities*, because if *Entity_1* and *Entity_2* are both present in a sentence, then *Entities* cannot be co-present. Conversely, *Entity_1* and *Entity_2* stand in a *Requires* relationship, because the first cannot occur without the second. This kind of information can clearly be helpful in case we have to automatically decide whether an argument is implicit or is just not present because it is not required.

INI/DNI preference Ruppenhofer and Michaelis (2009) suggest that omissible arguments in particular frames tend to be always interpreted as definite or indefinite. For example, they report that in a sample from the British National Corpus, the interpretation for a null instantiated *Goal* argument is definite in 97.5% of the observed cases. We take this feature into account by considering the frequency of an implicit argument being annotated as definite/indefinite in the training set.

The algorithm incorporating all this linguistic information is detailed in the following subsection.

4.1 INI/DNI identification

In a preliminary step, we collect for each frame the list of arguments being annotated as DNI/INI with the corresponding frequency in the training set. For example, in the CALENDRIC_UNIT frame, the *Whole* argument has been annotated 11 times as INI and 5 times as DNI. Some implicit frame elements occur only as INI or DNI, for example *Goal*, which is annotated 14 times as DNI and never as INI in the ARRIVING frame. This frequency list ($FreqList$) is collected in order to decide if candidate null instantiations have to be classified as DNI or INI.

We consider each sentence in the test data provided with FrameNet annotation, and for each predicate p annotated with a set of overt frame elements FEs, we run the first module for DNI/INI identification. The steps followed are reported in Algorithm 1. We first check if the annotated FEs contain all core frame elements C listed in FrameNet for p. If the two sets are identical, we conclude that no core frame element can be implicit and we return an empty set both for DNI and INI. For example, in the test sentence (6), the BODY_MOVEMENT frame appears in the sentence with its two core frame elements, i.e. *Body_part* and *Agent*. Therefore, no implicit argument can be postulated.

(6) Finally [she]$_{Agent}$ opened$_{BODY_MOVEMENT}$ [her eyes]$_{Body\_part}$ again.

If the core FEs in C are not all overtly expressed in FEs, we run two routines to check if the missing FEs $CandNIs$ are likely to be null instantiated elements. First, we discard all candidate NIs that appear as incorporated FEs for the given p. Second, we discard as well candidate NIs if they are excluded by the overtly annotated FEs.

The last steps of the algorithm are devoted to deciding if the candidate null instantiation is definite or indefinite. For this step, we rely on the observations collected in $FreqList$. In particular, for each candidate c we check if it was already present as INI or DNI in the training set. If yes, we label c accordingly. In case c was observed both as INI and as DNI, the most probable label is assigned based on its frequency in the training set.

```
Input: TestSet with annotated core FEs;
       FreqList
Output: INI and DNI for p
foreach p ∈ TestSet do
    extract annotated core FEs;
    extract set C of core FEs for p in FrameNet;
    if C ⊆ FEs then
        DNI = ∅;
        INI = ∅;
    else
        C \ FEs = CandNIs;
        foreach c ∈ CandNIs do
            if c is incorporated FE of p then
                delete c
            foreach fe ∈ FEs do
                if fe excludes c then
                    delete c
            end
            foreach ni_p ∈ FreqList_p do
                if c = ni_p then
                    if ni_p is_only dni_p then
                        c ∈ DNI
                    if ni_p is_only ini_p then
                        c ∈ INI
                    if ni_p is ini_p and ni_p is dni_p
                    then
                        if Freq(ini_p) >
                        Freq(dni_p) then
                            c ∈ INI
                        else
                            c ∈ DNI
            end
        end
    return(INI);
    return(DNI);
end
```

Algorithm 1: DNI/INI identification

4.2 DNI binding

Given that both the supervised approach exploited by Chen et al. (2010) and the methodology proposed in Tonelli and Delmonte (2010) based on deep-semantic parsing achieved quite poor results in the DNI-binding task, we devise a third approach that relies on the observed heads of each FE in the training set and assigns a relevance score to each candidate antecedent.

We first collect for each FE the list of heads H_{train} assigned to FE in the training set, and we extract for each head $h_{train} \in H_{train}$ the corresponding frequency $f_{h_{train}}$. Then, for each $dni \in DNI$ identified with Algorithm 1 in the test set, we collect all nominal heads H_{test} occurring in a window of (plus/minus) 5 sentences and we assign to each candidate head $h_{test} \in H_{test}$ a relevance score $rel_{h_{test}}$ w.r.t. dni computed as follows:

$$rel_{h_{test}} = \frac{f_{h_{train}}}{dist(sent_{dni}, sent_{h_{test}})} \qquad (7)$$

where $f_{h_{train}}$ is the number of times h has been observed in the training set with a FE label, and $dist(sent_{dni}, sent_{h_{test}})$ is the distance between the sentence where the dni has been detected and the sentence where the candidate head h_{test} occurs ($0 \leq dist(sent_{dni}, sent_{h_{test}}) \leq 5$).

The best candidate head for dni is the one with the highest $rel_{h_{test}}$, given that it is (higher) than 0. The way we compute the relevance score is based on the intuition that, if a head was frequently observed for FE in the training set, it is likely that it is a good candidate. However, the more distant it occurs from dni, then less probable it is as antecedent.

5 Evaluation and error analysis

We present here an evaluation of the system output on test data. We further comment on some difficult aspects of the task and suggest some solutions.

5.1 Results

Evaluation consists of different layers, which we consider separately. The first task was to decide whether an argument is implicit or not. We were able to identify 53.8% of all null instantiated arguments in text, which is lower than the recall of 63.4% achieved by SEMAFOR (Chen et al., 2010), the best performing system in the challenge. However, in the following subtask of deciding whether an implicit argument is an INI or a DNI, we achieved an accuracy of 74.6% (vs. 54.7% of SEMAFOR, even if our result is based on fewer proposed classifications). Note that the majority-class accuracy reported by Ruppenhofer et al. (2010) is 50.8%.

In Table 2 we further report precision, recall and F1 scores computed separately on all DNIs and all INIs automatically detected. Precision corresponds to the percentage of null instantiations found (either INI or DNI) that are correctly labeled as such, while recall indicates the amount of INI or DNI that were correctly identified compared to the gold standard ones. Our approach does not show significant differences between the result obtained with INIs and DNIs, while the evaluation of SEMAFOR (between parenthesis) shows that its performance suffers from low recall as regards DNIs and low precision as regards INIs.

	P	R	F1
DNI	0.39 (0.57)	0.43 (0.03)	0.41 (0.06)
INI	0.46 (0.20)	0.38 (0.61)	0.42 (0.30)

Table 2: Evaluation of INI/DNI identification. SEMAFOR performance between parenthesis.

Another evaluation step concerns the binding of DNIs with the corresponding antecedents by applying the equation reported in Section 4.2. Results are shown in Table 3:

	P	R	F1
DNI	0.13 (0.25)	0.06 (0.01)	0.08 (0.02)

Table 3: Evaluation of DNI resolution. SEMAFOR performance between parenthesis.

Although the binding quality still needs to be improved, two main factors have a negative impact on our performance, which do not depend on our algorithm: first, 9% of the DNIs we bound to an antecedent don't have a referent in the gold standard. Second, 26% of the wrong assignments concern antecedents found for the *Topic* frame element in test sentences where the STATEMENT frame has been annotated together with the overtly expressed core FE *Message*. In all these gold cases, *Topic* is not considered null instantiated if the *Message* FE is explicit in the clause. Therefore, we can conclude that the mistake done by our algorithm depends on the missing *Excludes* relation between *Topic* and *Message*, i.e. a rule should be introduced saying that one of the two roles is redundant (and not null instantiated) if the other is overtly expressed.

5.2 Open issues related to our approach

Even if with a small set of rules our approach achieved state-of-the-art results in the SemEval task, our performance clearly requires further improvements. Indeed, we currently rely only on the background knowledge about core FEs from FrameNet, combined with statistical observations about role fillers acquired from the training set. Additional morphological, syntactic, semantic and discourse information could be exploited in different ways. For example, since the passive voice of a verb can constructionally license INIs, this kind of information would greatly improve our performance with verbal predicates (i.e. 46% of all annotated predicates in the test set).

As for nominal predicates, consider for example sentence (8) extracted from the test set:

(8) 'Excuse the admiration$_{\text{JUDGMENT}}$ [of a connoisseur]$_{\text{Evaluee}}$,' said [he]$_{\text{Cognizer}}$.

In this case, 'admiration' is a nominal predicate with two explicit FEs, namely *Evaluee* and *Cognizer*. The JUDGMENT frame includes also the *Reason* core FE, which can be a candidate for a null instantiation. In fact, it is annotated as INI in the gold standard data, because in the previous sentences a reason for such admiration is not mentioned. However, this could have been annotated as DNI as well, if only some specific quality of the person had been previously introduced. This shows that the current sentence does not present any inherent characteristic motivating the presence of a definite instantiation. In this case, a strategy based on some kind of history list may be very helpful. This could contain, for example, all subjects and direct objects previously mentioned in text and selected according to some relevance criteria, as in (Tonelli and Delmonte, 2010). A further improvement may derive from the integration of an anaphora resolution step, as first proposed by Palmer et al. (1986) and more recently by Gerber and Chai (2010).

5.3 Open issues related to the task

Other open issues are related to the specification of the task and to the nature of implicit entities, which make it difficult to account for this phenomenon from a computational point of view. We report below the main issues that need to be tackled:

INI Linking: Table 1 shows that 28% of DNIs in the test set are not linked to any referent. This puts into question one of the main assumptions of the task, that is the connection between a definite instantiation and a referent. In the test set, there are also 14 cases of indefinite null instantiations (out of 361) that are provided with a referent. Consider for example the following sentence with gold standard annotation, in which the INI label *Path* is actually instantiated and refers to 'we':

(9) (We)$_{\text{Path}}$ allowed [him]$_{\text{Theme}}$ to pass$_{\text{TRAVERSING}}$ before we had recovered our nerve.

This again may be a controversial annotation choice, since the annotation guidelines of the task reported that '*in cases of indefinite omission, there need not be any overt mention of an indefinite NP in the linguistic context nor does there have to be a referent of the kind denoted by the omitted argument in the physical discourse setting*' (Ruppenhofer, 2010).

Position of referent: Although we suggested that the History List may represent a good starting point for finding antecedents to DNIs, searching only in the context *preceding* the current predicate is not enough because the referent can occur *after* such predicate. Also, the predicate with a DNI and the referent can be divided by a very large text span. In the test data, 38% of the DNIs referent occur in the same sentence of the predicate, while 14% are mentioned after that (in a text span of max. 4 sentences). Another 38% of DNIs are resolved in a text span preceding the current predicate of max. 5 sentences, while the rest has a very far antecedent (up to 116 sentences before the current predicate). The notion of context where the antecedent should be searched for is clearly lacking an appropriate definition.

Diversity of lexical fillers: In general, it is possible to successfully obtain information about the likely fillers of a missing FE from annotated data sets only in case all FE labels are semantically well identifiable: in fact many FE labels are devoid of any specific associated meaning. Furthermore, lexical fillers of a given semantic role in the FrameNet data sets can be as diverse as possible. For example, a complete search in the FrameNet database for the FE Charges will reveal heads like 'possession, innocent, actions', where the significant portion of text addressed by the FE would be in the specification - i.e. 'possession of a gun' etc. Only in case of highly specialized FEs there will be some help in the semantic characterization of a possible antecedent.

6 Conclusions

In this paper, we have described the phenomenon of null instantiated arguments according to the FrameNet paradigm and we have proposed a strategy for identifying implicit arguments and finding their antecedents, if any, using a linguistically-motivated approach. We have evaluated our system using the test set developed for the SemEval task 10 and we have discussed some problems in our approach affecting its performance. Besides, we have also pointed out some issues related to the task definition and to the general phenomenon of null instantiated arguments that make the identification task challenging from a computational point of view. We have shed some light on the syntactic, semantic and discourse information that we believe are necessary to successfully handle the task.

In the future, we plan to improve on our binding approach by making our model more flexible. More specifically, we currently treat DNI referents occurring before and after the sentence containing the predicate as equally probable. Instead, we should penalize less those *preceding* the predicate because they are more frequent in the training set. For this reason, the number of observations for the candidate head and the distance should be represented as different weighted features. Another direction to explore is to extend the training set to the whole FrameNet resource and not just to the SemEval data set. However, our approach based on the observations of lexical fillers is very much domain-dependent, and a larger training set may introduce too much variability in the heads. An approach exploiting some kind of generalization, for example by linking the fillers to WordNet synsets as proposed by (Gerber and Chai, 2010), may be more appropriate.

References

Collin F. Baker, Charles J. Fillmore, and J. B. Lowe. 1998. The Berkeley FrameNet Project. In *Proceedings of Coling/ACL*, Montreal, Quebec, Canada.

C. F. Baker, M. Ellsworth, and K. Erk. 2007. Semeval-2007 task 10: Frame semantic structure extraction. In *Proceedings of the Fourth International Workshop on Semantic Evaluations (SemEval-2007)*, pages 99–104, Prague, CZ, June.

Aljoscha Burchardt, Annette Frank, and Manfred Pinkal. 2005. Building text meaning representations from contextually related frames - a case study. In *Proceedings of the Sixth International Workshop on Computational Semantics*, Tilburg, NL.

Desai Chen, Nathan Schneider, Dipanjan Das, and Noah A. Smith. 2010. SEMAFOR: Frame Argument Resolution with Log-Linear Models. In *Proceedings of SemEval-2010: 5th International Workshop on Semantic Evaluations*, pages 264–267, Uppsala, Sweden. Association for Computational Linguistics.

Rodolfo Delmonte. 2009. Understanding Implicit Entities and Events with Getaruns. In *Proceedings of the IEEE International Conference on Semantic Computing*, pages 25–32, Berkeley, California.

Charles J. Fillmore. 1986. Pragmatically Controlled Zero Anaphora. In V. Nikiforidou, M. Vanllay, M. Niepokuj, and D. Felder, editors, *Proceedings of the XII Annual Meeting of the Berkeley Linguistics Society*, Berkeley, California. BLS.

Matthew Gerber and Joyce Y. Chai. 2010. Beyond NomBank: A Study of Implicit Arguments for Nominal Predicates. In *Proceedings of the 48th annual meeting of the Association for Computational Linguistics (ACL-10)*, pages 1583–1592, Uppsala, Sweden. Association for Computational Linguistics.

Adam Meyers. 2007. Annotation guidelines for NomBank - noun argument structure for PropBank. Technical report, New York University.

M. Palmer, D. Dahl, R. Passonneau, L. Hirschman, M. Linebarger, and J. Dowding. 1986. Recovering implicit information. In *Proceedings of ACL 1986*, pages 96–113.

Martha Palmer, Daniel Gildea, and Paul Kingsbury. 2005. The Proposition Bank: An Annotated Corpus of Semantic Roles. *Computational Linguistics*, 31.

Josef Ruppenhofer and Laura A. Michaelis. 2009. Frames predict the interpretation of lexical omissions. Submitted.

Josef Ruppenhofer, Caroline Sporleder, Roser Morante, Collin F. Baker, and Martha Palmer. 2010. SemEval-2010 Task 10: Linking Events and Their Participants in Discourse. In *Proceedings of SemEval-2010: 5th International Workshop on Semantic Evaluations*.

Josef Ruppenhofer, 2010. *Annotation guidelines used for Semeval task 10 - Linking Events and Their Participants in Discourse*. (manuscript).

Sara Tonelli and Rodolfo Delmonte. 2010. VENSES++: Adapting a deep semantic processing system to the identification of null instantiations. In *Proceedings of SemEval-2010: 5th International Workshop on Semantic Evaluations*, Uppsala, Sweden.

A Joint Model of Implicit Arguments for Nominal Predicates

Matthew Gerber and **Joyce Y. Chai**
Department of Computer Science
Michigan State University
East Lansing, Michigan, USA
{gerberm2, jchai}@cse.msu.edu

Robert Bart
Computer Science and Engineering
University of Washington
Seattle, Washington, USA
rbart@cs.washington.edu

Abstract

Many prior studies have investigated the recovery of semantic arguments for nominal predicates. The models in many of these studies have assumed that arguments are independent of each other. This assumption simplifies the computational modeling of semantic arguments, but it ignores the joint nature of natural language. This paper presents a preliminary investigation into the joint modeling of implicit arguments for nominal predicates. The joint model uses propositional knowledge extracted from millions of Internet webpages to help guide prediction.

1 Introduction

Much recent work on semantic role labeling has focused on joint models of arguments. This work is motivated by the fact that one argument can either promote or inhibit the presence of another argument. Because most of this work has been done for verbal SRL, nominal SRL has lagged behind somewhat. In particular, the "implicit" nominal SRL model created by Gerber and Chai (2010) does not address joint argument structures. Implicit arguments are similar to standard SRL arguments, a primary difference being their ability to cross sentence boundaries. In the model created by Gerber and Chai, implicit argument candidates are classified independently and a heuristic post-processing method is applied to derive the final structure. This paper presents a preliminary joint implicit argument model.

Consider the following sentences:[1]

(1) [c_1 The president] is currently struggling to manage [c_2 the country's economy].

(2) If he cannot get it under control, [p loss] of [arg_1 the next election] might result.

In Example 2, we are searching for the $iarg_0$ of *loss* (the entity that is losing). The sentence in Example 1 supplies two candidates c_1 and c_2. If one only considers the predicate *loss*, then c_1 and c_2 would both be reasonable fillers for the $iarg_0$: presidents often lose things (e.g., votes and allegiance) and economies often lose things (e.g., jobs and value). However, the sentence in Example 2 supplies additional information. It tells the reader that *the next election* is the entity being lost. Given this information, one would likely prefer c_1 over c_2 because economies don't generally lose elections, whereas presidents often do. This type of inference is common in textual discourses because authors assume a shared knowledge base with their readers. This knowledge base contains information about events and their typical participants (e.g., the fact that presidents lose elections but economies do not).

The model presented in this paper relies on a knowledge base constructed by automatically mining semantic propositions from Internet webpages. These propositions help to identify likely joint implicit argument configurations. In the following section, we review work on joint inference within semantic role labeling. In Sections 4 and 5, we present the joint implicit argument model and its features. Evaluation results for this model are given in Sec-

[1] We will use the notation of Gerber and Chai (2010), where standard nominal arguments are indicated with arg_n and implicit arguments are indicated with $iarg_n$.

tion 6. The joint model contains many simplifying assumptions, which we address in Section 7. We conclude in Section 8.

2 Related work

A number of recent studies have shown that semantic arguments are not independent and that system performance can be improved by taking argument dependencies into account. Consider the following examples, due to Toutanova et al. (2008):

(3) [*Temporal* The day] that [arg_0 the ogre] [*Predicate* cooked] [arg_1 the children] is still remembered.

(4) [arg_1 The meal] that [arg_0 the ogre] [*Predicate* cooked] [*Beneficiary* the children] is still remembered.

These examples demonstrate the importance of inter-argument dependencies. The change from *day* in Example 3 to *meal* in Example 4 affects more than just the *Temporal* label: additionally, the arg_1 changes to *Beneficiary*, even though the underlying text (*the children*) does not change. To capture this dependency, Toutanova el al. first generate an n-best list of argument labels for a predicate instance. They then re-rank this list using joint features that describe multiple arguments simultaneously. The features help prevent globally invalid argument configurations (e.g., ones with multiple arg_0 labels).

Punyakanok et al. (2008) formulate a variety of constraints on argument configurations. For example, arguments are not allowed to overlap the predicate, nor are they allowed to overlap each other. The authors treat these constraints as binary variables within an integer linear program, which is optimized to produce the final labeling.

Ritter et al. (2010) investigated joint selectional preferences. Traditionally, a selectional preference model provides the strength of association between a predicate-argument position and a specific textual expression. Returning to Examples 1 and 2, one sees that the selectional preference for *president* and *economy* in the $iarg_0$ position of *loss* should be high. Ritter et al. extended this single-argument model using a joint formulation of Latent Dirichlet Allocation (LDA) (Blei et al., 2003). In the generative version of joint LDA, text for the argument positions is generated from a common hidden variable. This approach reflects the intuition behind Examples 1 and 2 and would help identify *president* as the $iarg_0$. Training data for the model was drawn from a large corpus of two-argument tuples extracted by the TextRunner system, which we describe next.

Both Ritter et al.'s model and the model described in this paper rely heavily on information extracted by the TextRunner system (Banko et al., 2007). The TextRunner system extracts tuples from Internet webpages in an unsupervised fashion. One key difference between TextRunner and other information extraction systems is that TextRunner does not use a closed set of relations (compare to the work described by ACE (2008)). Instead, the relation set is left open, leading to the notion of Open Information Extraction (OIE). Although OIE often has lower precision than traditional information extraction, it is able to extract a wider variety of relations at precision levels that are often useful (Banko and Etzioni, 2008).

3 Using TextRunner to assess joint argument assignments

Returning again to Examples 1 and 2, one can query TextRunner in the following way:

arg_0 : ?

Predicate : lose[2]

arg_1 : election

In the TextRunner system, arg_0 typically indicates the *Agent* and arg_1 typically indicates the *Theme*. TextRunner provides many tuples in response to this query, two of which are shown below:

(5) Usually, [arg_0 the president's party] [*Predicate* loses] [arg_1 seats in the mid-term election].

(6) [arg_0 The president] [*Predicate* lost] [arg_1 the election].

The tuples present in these sentences give strong indicators about the type of entity that loses elections.

[2]Nominal predicates are mapped to their verbal forms using information provided by the NomBank lexicon.

Given all of the returned tuples, only a single one involves *economy* in the arg_0 position:

(7) Any president will take credit for [arg_0 a good economy] or [*Predicate* lose] [arg_1 an election] over a bad one.

In Example 7, TextRunner has not analyzed the arguments correctly (*president* should be the arg_0, not *economy*).[3] In Section 5, we show how evidence from the tuple lists can be aggregated such that correct analyses (5 and 6) are favored over incorrect analyses (7). The primary contribution of this paper is an exploration of how the aggregated evidence can be used to identify implicit arguments (e.g., *president* in Example 1).

4 Joint model formulation

To simplify the experimental setting, the model described in this paper targets the specific situation where a predicate instance *p* takes an implicit $iarg_0$ and an implicit $iarg_1$.[4] Whereas the model proposed by Gerber and Chai (2010) classifies candidates for these positions independently, the model in this paper classifies joint structures by evaluating the following binary prediction function:

$$P(+| \langle p, iarg_0, c_i, iarg_1, c_j \rangle) \quad (8)$$

Equation 8 gives the probability of the joint assignment of c_i to $iarg_0$ and c_j to $iarg_1$. Given a set of n candidates $c_1, \ldots, c_n \in C$, the best labeling is found by considering all possible assignments of c_i and c_j:

$$\underset{(c_i, c_j) \in C \text{x} C \text{ s.t. } i \neq j}{\arg\max} \quad P(+| \langle p, iarg_0, c_i, iarg_1, c_j \rangle) \quad (9)$$

Consider modified versions of Examples 1 and 2:

(10) [c_1 The president] is currently struggling to manage [c_2 the country's economy].

(11) If he cannot get it under control before [c_3 the next election], a [p loss] might result.

[3]Banko and Etzioni (2008) cite a precision score of 88% for their system.

[4]This simplifying assumption does not hold for real data, and is addressed further in Section 7.2.

In this case, we are looking for the $iarg_0$ as well as the $iarg_1$ for the *loss* predicate. Three candidates c_1, c_2, and c_3 are marked. The joint model would evaluate the following probabilities, taking the highest scoring to be the final assignment:

$$P(+| \langle \text{loss}, iarg_0, \text{president}, iarg_1, \text{economy} \rangle)$$
$$*P(+| \langle \text{loss}, iarg_0, \text{president}, iarg_1, \text{election} \rangle)$$
$$P(+| \langle \text{loss}, iarg_0, \text{economy}, iarg_1, \text{president} \rangle)$$
$$P(+| \langle \text{loss}, iarg_0, \text{economy}, iarg_1, \text{election} \rangle)$$
$$P(+| \langle \text{loss}, iarg_0, \text{election}, iarg_1, \text{president} \rangle)$$
$$P(+| \langle \text{loss}, iarg_0, \text{election}, iarg_1, \text{economy} \rangle)$$

Intuitively, only the starred item should have a high probability. In the following section, we describe how these probabilities can be estimated using information extracted by TextRunner.

5 Joint model features

As mentioned in Section 2, the TextRunner system has been extracting massive amounts of knowledge in the form of tuples such as the following:

$$\langle \text{president}, \text{lose}, \text{election} \rangle$$

The database of tuples can be queried by supplying one or more of the tuple arguments. For example, the following is a partial result list for the query ⟨president, lose, ?⟩:

⟨Kenyan president, lose, election⟩
⟨president's party, lose seat in, election⟩
⟨president, lose, ally⟩

The final position in each of these tuples (e.g., *election*) provides a single answer to the question "What might a president lose?". Aggregation begins by generalizing each answer to its WordNet synset (glosses are shown after the arrows):

⟨Kenyan president, lose, election⟩ → a vote
⟨president's party, lose seat in, election⟩ (same)
⟨president, lose, ally⟩ → friendly nation

In cases where a tuple argument has multiple WordNet senses, the tuple is mapped to the most common sense as listed in the WordNet database.

Having mapped each tuple to its synset, each synset is ranked according to the number of tuples that it covers. For the query $\langle$president, lose, ?$\rangle$, this produces the following ranked list of WordNet synsets (only the top five are shown, with the number in parentheses indicating how many tuples are covered):

1. election (77)
2. war (51)
3. vote (39)
4. people (34)
5. support (26)

...

The synsets above indicate likely answers to the previous question of "What might a president lose?".

In a similar manner, one can answer a question such as "What might lose an election?" using tuples extracted by TextRunner. The procedure described above produces the following ranked list of WordNet synsets to answer this question:

...

9. people (62)
10. Republican (51)
11. Republican party (51)
12. Hillary (50)
13. president (49)

...

In this case, the expected answer (*president*) ranks 13th in the list of answer synsets. It is important to note that lower ranked answers are not necessarily incorrect answers. It is a simple fact that a wide variety of entities can lose an election. Items 9-13 are all reasonable answers to the original question of what might lose an election.

The two symmetric questions defined and answered above are closely connected to the implicit argument situation discussed in Examples 10 and 11. In Example 11, one is searching for the implicit $iarg_0$ and $iarg_1$ to the *loss* predicate. Candidates c_i and c_j that truly fill these positions should be compatible with questions in the following forms:

Question: What did c_i lose?

Answer: c_j

Question: What entity lost c_j?

Answer: c_i

If either of these question-answer pairs is not satisfied, then the joint assignment of c_i to $iarg_0$ and c_j to $iarg_1$ should be considered unlikely. Using the first question-answer pair above as an example, satisfaction is determined in the following way:

1. Query TextRunner for $\langle c_i, \text{lose}, ?\rangle$, retrieving the top n tuples.
2. Map the final argument of each tuple to its WordNet synset and rank the synsets by frequency, producing the ranked list A of answer synsets.
3. Map c_j to its most common WordNet synset $synset_{c_j}$ and determine whether $synset_{c_j}$ exists in A. If it does, the question-answer pair is satisfied.

Some additional processing is required to determine whether $synset_{c_j}$ exists in A. This is due to the hierarchical organization of WordNet. For example, suppose that $synset_{c_j}$ is the synset containing "primary election" and A contains synsets paraphrased as follows:

1. election
2. war
3. vote

...

$synset_{c_j}$ does not appear directly in this list; however, its existence in the list is implied by the following hypernymy path within WordNet:

$$\text{primary election} \xrightarrow{\text{is-a}} \text{election}$$

Intuitively, if $synset_{c_j}$ is connected to a highly ranked synset in A by a short path, then one has evidence that $synset_{c_j}$ answers the original question.

The evidence is weaker if the path is long, as in the following example:

$$\text{open primary} \xrightarrow{\text{is-a}} \text{direct primary} \xrightarrow{\text{is-a}} \text{primary election} \xrightarrow{\text{is-a}} \text{election}$$

Additionally, a path between more specific synsets (i.e., those lower in the hierarchy) indicates a stronger relationship than a path between more general synsets (i.e., those higher in the hierarchy). These two situations are depicted in Figure 1. The synset similarity metric defined by Wu and Palmer (1994) combines the path length and synset depth intuitions into a single numeric score that is defined as follows:

$$\frac{2 * depth(lca(synset_1, synset_2))}{depth(synset_1) + depth(synset_2)} \quad (12)$$

In Equation 12, *lca* returns the lowest common ancestor of the two synsets within the WordNet *is-a* hierarchy.

To summarize, Equation 12 indicates the strength of association between $synset_{c_j}$ (e.g., primary election) and a ranked synset $synset_a$ from A that answers a question such as "What might a president lose?". If the association between $synset_{c_j}$ and $synset_a$ is small, then the assignment of c_j to $iarg_1$ is unlikely. The process works similarly for assessing c_i as the filler of $iarg_0$. In what follows, we quantify this intuition with features used to represent the conditioning information in Equation 8.

Feature 1: Maximum association strength. Given the conditioning variables in Equation 8, there are two questions that can be asked:

Question: What did c_i p?

Answer: c_j

Question: What entity p c_j?

Answer: c_i

Each of these questions produces a ranked list of answer synsets using the approach described previously. The synset for each answer string will match zero or more of the answer synsets, and each of these matches will be associated with a similarity score as defined in Equation 12. Feature 1 considers all such similarity scores and selects the maximum. A high value for this feature indicates that one (or both) of the candidates (c_i or c_j) is likely to fill its associated implicit argument position.

Feature 2: Maximum reciprocal rank. Of all the answer matches described for Feature 1, Feature 2 selects the highest ranking and forms the reciprocal rank. Thus, values for Feature 2 are in [0,1] with larger values indicating matches with higher ranked answer synsets.

Feature 3: Number of matches. This feature records the total number of answer string matches from either of the questions described for Feature 1.

Feature 4: Sum reciprocal rank. Feature 2 considers answer synset matches from either of the posed questions; ideally, each question-answer pair should have some influence on the probability estimate in Equation 8. Feature 4 looks at the answer synset matches from each question individually. The match with highest rank for each question is selected, and the reciprocal rank $\frac{2}{r_1 + r_2}$ is computed. The value of this feature is zero if either of the questions fails to produce a matching answer synset.

Features 5 and 6: Local classification scores. The joint model described in this paper does not replace the local prediction model presented by Gerber and Chai (2010). The latter uses a wide variety of important features that cannot be ignored. Like previous joint models (e.g., the one described by Toutanova et al. (2008)), the joint model works on top of the local prediction model, whose scores are incorporated into the joint model as feature-value pairs. Given the local prediction scores for the $iarg_0$ and $iarg_1$ positions in Equation 8, the joint model forms two features: (1) the sum of the scores for c_i filling $iarg_0$ and c_j filling $iarg_1$, and (2) the product of these two scores.

6 Evaluation

We evaluated the joint model described in the previous sections over the manually annotated implicit

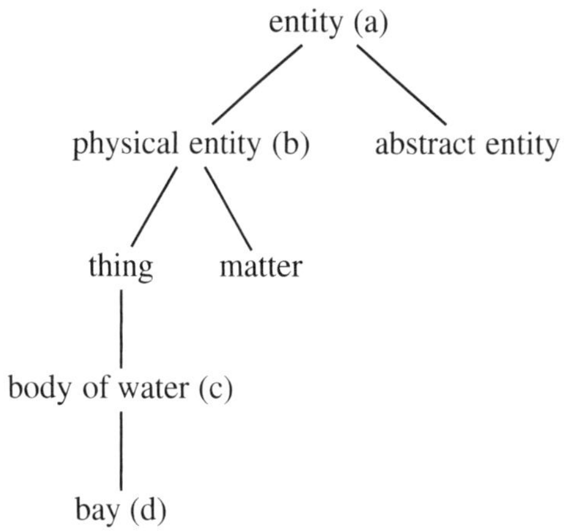

Figure 1: Effect of depth on WordNet synset similarity. All links indicate *is-a* relationships. Although the link distance from (a) to (b) equals the distance from (c) to (d), the latter are more similar due to their lower depth within the WordNet hierarchy.

argument data created by Gerber and Chai (2010). This dataset contains full-text implicit argument annotations for approximately 1,200 predicate instances within the Penn TreeBank. As mentioned in Section 4, all experiments were conducted using predicate instances that take an $iarg_0$ and $iarg_1$ in the ground-truth annotations. We used a tenfold cross-validation setup and the evaluation metrics proposed by Ruppenhofer et al. (2009), which were also used by Gerber and Chai. For each evaluation fold, features were selected using only the corresponding training data and the greedy selection algorithm proposed by Pudil et al. (1994), which starts with an empty feature set and incrementally adds features that provide the highest gains.

For comparison with Gerber and Chai's model, we also evaluated the local prediction model on the evaluation data. Because this model predicted implicit arguments independently, it continued to use the heuristic post-processing algorithm to arrive at the final labeling. However, the prediction threshold t was eliminated because the system could safely assume that a true filler for the $iarg_0$ and $iarg_1$ positions existed.

Table 1 presents the evaluation results. The first thing to note is that these results are not comparable to the results presented by Gerber and Chai (2010). In general, performance is much higher because predicate instances reliably take implicit arguments in the $iarg_0$ and $iarg_1$ positions. The overall performance increase versus the local model is relatively small (approximately 1 percentage point); however, the *bid* predicate in particular showed a substantial increase (greater than 11 percentage points).

7 Discussion

7.1 Example improvement versus local model

The *bid* and *investment* predicates showed the largest increase for the joint model versus the local model. Below, we give an example of the *investment* predicate for which the joint model correctly identified the $iarg_0$ and the local model did not.

(13) [Big investors] can decide to ride out market storms without jettisoning stock.

(14) Most often, [c they] do just that, because stocks have proved to be the best-performing long-term [*Predicate* investment], attracting about $1 trillion from pension funds alone.

Both models identified the $iarg_1$ as *money* from a prior sentence (not shown). The local model incorrectly predicted *$1 trillion* in Example 14 as the $iarg_0$ for the *investment* event. This mistake demonstrates a fundamental limitation of the local model: it cannot detect simple incompatibilities in the predicted argument structure. It does not know that "money investing money" is a rare or impossible event in the real world.

For the joint model's prediction, consider the constituent marked with c in Example 14. This con-

		Local model			Joint model		
	# Imp. args.	P	R	F_1	P	R	F_1
price	40	65.0	65.0	65.0	67.5	67.5	67.5
sale	34	86.5	86.5	86.5	84.3	84.3	84.3
plan	30	60.0	60.0	60.0	56.7	56.7	56.7
bid	26	66.7	66.7	66.7	78.2	78.2	78.2
fund	18	83.3	83.3	83.3	83.3	83.3	83.3
loss	14	100.0	100.0	100.0	100.0	100.0	100.0
loan	12	63.6	58.3	60.9	50.0	50.0	50.0
investment	8	57.1	50.0	53.3	62.5	62.5	62.5
Overall	182	72.6	71.8	72.2	73.1	73.1	73.1

Table 1: Joint implicit argument evaluation results. The second column gives the total number of implicit arguments in the ground-truth annotations. P, R, and F_1 indicate precision, recall, and f-measure ($\beta = 1$) as defined by Ruppenhofer et al. (2009).

stituent is resolved to *Big investors* in the preceding sentence. Thus, the two relevant questions are as follows:

Question: What did big investors invest?

Answer: money

Question: What entity invested money?

Answer: big investors

The first question produces the following ranked list of answer synsets (the number in parentheses indicates the number of answer tuples mapped to the synset):

money (71)

amount (38)

million (38)

billion (22)

capital (21)

As shown, the answer string of *money* matches the top-ranked answer synset. The second question produces the following ranked list of answer synsets:

company (642)

people (460)

government (275)

business (75)

investor (70)

In this case, the answer string *Big investors* matches the fifth answer synset. The combined evidence of these two question-answer pairs allows the joint system to successfully identify *Big investors* as the $iarg_0$ of the *investment* predicate in Example 14.

7.2 Toward a generally applicable joint model

The joint model presented in this paper assumes that all predicate instances take an $iarg_0$ and $iarg_1$. This assumption clearly does not hold for real data (these positions are often not expressed in the text), but relaxing it will require investigation of the following issues:

1. **Explicit arguments** should also be considered when determining whether a candidate c fills an implicit argument position $iarg_n$. The motivation here is similar to that given elsewhere in this paper: arguments (whether implicit or explicit) are not independent. This is demonstrated by Example 2 at the beginning of this paper, where *election* is an explicit argument to the predicate and affects the implicit argument inference. The model developed in this paper only considers jointly occurring implicit arguments.

2. **Other implicit argument positions (e.g., $iarg_2$, $iarg_3$, etc.)** need to be accounted for as well. This will present a challenge when it comes to extracting the necessary

propositions from TextRunner. Currently, TextRunner only handles tuples of the form $\langle arg_0, p, arg_1 \rangle$. Other argument positions are not directly analyzed by the system; however, because TextRunner also returns the sentence from which a tuple is extracted, these additional argument positions could be extracted in the following way:

(a) For an instance of the *sale* predicate with an arg_0 of *company*, to find likely arg_2 fillers (the entity purchasing the item), query TextRunner with $\langle \text{company}, sell, ? \rangle$.
(b) Perform standard verbal SRL on the sentences for the resulting tuples, identifying any arg_2 occurrences.
(c) Cluster and rank the arg_2 fillers according to the method described in this paper.

This approach combines Open Information Extraction with traditional information extraction (i.e., verbal SRL).

3. **Computational complexity and probability estimation** is a problem for many joint models. The model presented in this paper quickly becomes computationally intractable when the number of candidates and implicit argument positions becomes moderately large. This is because Equation 9 considers all possible assignments of candidates to implicit argument positions. With as few as thirty candidates and five argument positions (not uncommon), one must evaluate $30!/25! = 17,100,720$ possible assignments. Although this particular formulation is not tractable, one based on dynamic programming or heuristic search might give reasonable results. Efficient estimation of the joint probability via Gibbs sampling would also be a possible approach (Resnik and Hardisty, 2010).

8 Conclusions

Many prior studies have investigated the recovery of semantic arguments for nominal predicates. The models in many of these studies have assumed that the arguments are independent of each other. This assumption simplifies the computational modeling of semantic arguments, but it ignores the joint nature of natural language. In order to take advantage of the information provided by jointly occurring arguments, the independent prediction models must be enhanced.

This paper has presented a preliminary investigation into the joint modeling of implicit arguments for nominal predicates. The model relies heavily on information extracted by the TextRunner extraction system, which pulls propositional tuples from millions of Internet webpages. These tuples encode world knowledge that is necessary for resolving semantic arguments in general and implicit arguments in particular. This paper has proposed methods of aggregating tuple knowledge to guide implicit argument resolution. The aggregated knowledge is applied via a re-ranking model that operates on top of the local prediction model described in previous work.

The performance gain across all predicate instances is relatively small; however, larger gains are observed for the *bid* and *investment* predicates. The improvement in Example 14 shows that the joint model is capable of correcting a bad local prediction using information extracted by the TextRunner system. This type of information is not used by the local prediction model.

Although the results in this paper show that some improvement is possible through the use of a joint model of implicit arguments, a significant amount of future work will be required to make the model widely applicable.

References

ACE, 2008. *The ACE 2008 Evaluation Plan*. NIST, 1.2d edition, August.

Michele Banko and Oren Etzioni. 2008. The tradeoffs between open and traditional relation extraction. In *Proceedings of ACL-08: HLT*, pages 28–36, Columbus, Ohio, June. Association for Computational Linguistics.

Michele Banko, Michael J Cafarella, Stephen Soderland, Matt Broadhead, and Oren Etzioni. 2007. Open information extraction from the web. In *Proceedings of the 20th International Joint Conference on Artificial Intelligence*.

David M. Blei, Andrew Y. Ng, and Michael I. Jordan.

2003. Latent dirichlet allocation. *J. Mach. Learn. Res.*, 3:993–1022.

Matthew Gerber and Joyce Chai. 2010. Beyond NomBank: A study of implicit arguments for nominal predicates. In *Proceedings of the 48th Annual Meeting of the Association for Computational Linguistics*, pages 1583–1592, Uppsala, Sweden, July. Association for Computational Linguistics.

P. Pudil, J. Novovicova, and J. Kittler. 1994. Floating search methods in feature selection. *Pattern Recognition Letters*, 15:1119–1125.

Vasin Punyakanok, Dan Roth, and Wen-tau Yih. 2008. The importance of syntactic parsing and inference in semantic role labeling. *Comput. Linguist.*, 34(2):257–287.

Philip Resnik and Eric Hardisty. 2010. Gibbs sampling for the uninitiated. Technical report, University of Maryland, June.

Alan Ritter, Mausam, and Oren Etzioni. 2010. A latent dirichlet allocation method for selectional preferences. In *Proceedings of the 48th Annual Meeting of the Association for Computational Linguistics*.

Josef Ruppenhofer, Caroline Sporleder, Roser Morante, Collin Baker, and Martha Palmer. 2009. Semeval-2010 task 10: Linking events and their participants in discourse. In *Proceedings of the Workshop on Semantic Evaluations: Recent Achievements and Future Directions (SEW-2009)*, pages 106–111, Boulder, Colorado, June. Association for Computational Linguistics.

Kristina Toutanova, Aria Haghighi, and Christopher D. Manning. 2008. A global joint model for semantic role labeling. *Comput. Linguist.*, 34(2):161–191.

Zhibiao Wu and Martha Palmer. 1994. Verb semantics and lexical selection. In *Proceedings of the 32nd Annual Meeting of the Association for Computational Linguistics*, pages 133–138, Las Cruces, New Mexico, USA, June. Association for Computational Linguistics.

Incorporating Coercive Constructions into a Verb Lexicon

Claire Bonial*, Susan Windisch Brown*, Jena D. Hwang*, Christopher Parisien, Martha Palmer* and Suzanne Stevenson****
*Department of Linguistics, University of Colorado at Boulder
**Department of Computer Science, University of Toronto
{Claire.Bonial, Susan.Brown, hwangd, Martha.Palmer}@colorado.edu
{chris, suzanne}@cs.toronto.edu

Abstract

We take the first steps towards augmenting a lexical resource, VerbNet, with probabilistic information about coercive constructions. We focus on CAUSED-MOTION as an example construction occurring with verbs for which it is a typical usage or for which it must be interpreted as extending the event semantics through coercion, which occurs productively and adds substantially to the relational semantics of a verb. However, through annotation we find that VerbNet fails to accurately capture all usages of the construction. We use unsupervised methods to estimate probabilistic measures from corpus data for predicting usage of the construction across verb classes in the lexicon and evaluate against VerbNet. We discuss how these methods will form the basis for enhancements for VerbNet supporting more accurate analysis of the relational semantics of a verb across productive usages.

1 Introduction

Automatic semantic analysis has been very successful when taking a supervised learning approach on data labeled with sense tags and semantic roles (e.g., see Màrquez et al., 2008). Underlying these recent successes are lexical resources, such as PropBank (Palmer et al., 2005), VerbNet (Kipper et al., 2008), and FrameNet (Baker et al., 1998; Fillmore et al., 2002), which encode the relational semantics of numerous lexical items, especially verbs. However, because authors and speakers use verbs productively in previously unseen ways, semantic analysis systems must not be limited to direct extrapolation from previously seen usages licensed by static lexical resources (cf. Pustejovsky & Jezek, 2008). To achieve more accurate semantic analyses, we must augment such resources with knowledge of the extensibility of verbs.

Central to verb extensibility is the process of semantic and syntactic coercion. Coercion allows a verb to be used in "atypical" contexts that extend its relational semantics, thereby enabling expression of a novel concept, or simply more fluid expression of a complex concept. For example, consider a strictly intransitive action verb such as *blink*. This verb may instead be used in a construction with an object, as in *She blinked the snow off her lashes*, leading to an interpretation of the verb in which the object is causally affected and changes location (the CAUSED-MOTION construction; Goldberg, 1995). This type of constructional coercion is common in language and underlies much extensibility of verb usages. Understanding such coercive processes thus has significant impact on how we should represent knowledge about verbs in a lexical resource.

Importantly, constructional coercion is not an all-or-nothing process – a word must be semantically and syntactically compatible in some respects with a context in order for its use to be extended to that context, but the restrictions on compatibility are not hard-and-fast rules (Langacker, 1987; Kay & Fillmore, 1999; Goldberg, 2006; Goldberg, to appear). Gradience of compatibility plays an important role in coercion, suggesting that a probabilistic approach may be necessary for encoding knowledge of constructional coercion in a verb lexicon (cf. Lapata & Lascarides, 2003).

Our hypothesis here is that, due to this gradient process of productivity, existing verb lexicons do not adequately capture the actual patterns of use of extensible constructions. In this paper, we focus on the CAUSED-MOTION (CM) construction as an initial test case. We first annotate the classes of an extensive verb lexicon, VerbNet, as to whether the CM construction is allowed for all, some, or none of the verbs in the class, noting additionally whether it is a typical or coerced usage. We find that many of the classes that allow the construction for at least some verbs do not include the CM frame in their definition, indicating a significant shortcoming in the relational knowledge encoded in the lexicon. Next, we develop probabilistic measures for determining to what degree a class is likely to admit the CM construction. We then test our measures over corpus data, manually annotated for use of the CM construction. Finally, we present preliminary work on automatic techniques for calculating the proposed measures in an unsupervised way, to avoid the need for expensive manual annotation. This work forms the preliminary steps toward empirically augmenting VerbNet's predictive capabilities concerning the event semantics of verbs in coercible constructions.

2 Extensible Constructions and VerbNet

Construction grammar has much insight to offer on the topic of productivity and on the resulting statistical patterns and gradience of usages (e.g., Langacker, 1987; Kay & Fillmore, 1999; Goldberg, 2006). A construction is formally defined to be any pairing of linguistic form (e.g., a syntactic frame) and meaning. Words can be used in constructions to the extent that their lexical semantics is compatible with – or can be coerced to be compatible with – the semantic constraints on the construction.

It is this notion of constructional coercion, and degree of coercibility, that accounts for the richness of usages that go beyond those thought of as typical or definitional for a verb: by coercing a verb not normally associated with a particular frame to occur in it, the meaning of the event can take on additional properties not considered a core part of the verb's semantics. For example, in the case of the sentence discussed above, *She blinked the snow off her lashes*, it is not the verb but rather the CM construction itself that licenses the direct object and adds the notion of "motion causally affecting the object" to the event semantics. Amongst other examples of well-known constructional coercions are: (1) The CAUSE-RECEIVE construction has the syntactic form of NP-V-NP-NP. For example, in *Bob painted Sally a picture*, the simple transitive verb *paint* gains the CAUSE TO RECEIVE sense, in which Sally is the recipient and the picture is the transferred item. (2) The WAY construction has the form of NP-V-[POSS *way*]-PP. For example, in *Frank found his way to New York*, the construction allows the verb *find* to gain a motion reading (i.e., "Frank traveled to New York") that would not otherwise be allowed (e.g., **Frank found to New York*).

Recognizing such extensions to the relational semantics of verbs is very important for accurate semantic interpretation in NLP. However, precise specifications for capturing the notion of coercible constructions, such as are needed for a computational resource, have heretofore been lacking.

2.1 VerbNet & Knowledge of Constructions

Computational verb lexicons are key to supporting NLP systems aimed at semantic interpretation. Verbs express the semantics of an event being described as well as the relational information among participants in that event, and project the syntactic structures that encode that information. Verbs are also highly variable, displaying a rich range of semantic and syntactic behavior.

Verb classifications help NLP systems to deal with this complexity by organizing verbs into groups that share core semantic and syntactic properties. For example, VerbNet (derived from Levin's [1993] work, Kipper et al., 2008) is widely used for a number of semantic processing tasks, including semantic role labeling (Swier and Stevenson, 2004), the creation of semantic parse trees (Shi and Mihalcea, 2005), and implicit argument resolution (Gerber and Chai, 2010). The detailed semantic predicates listed with each VerbNet class also have the potential to contribute to text-specific semantic representations and, thereby, to tasks requiring inferencing (Zaenen et al., 2008; Palmer et al., 2009).

VerbNet identifies semantic roles and syntactic patterns characteristic of the verbs in each class makes explicit the connections between the syntactic patterns and the underlying semantic relations that can be inferred for all members of the class. Each syntactic frame in a class has a corresponding semantic representation that details the semantic relations between event participants across the course of the event. For example, one of the characteristic patterns listed for the Pour class is a CAUSED-MOTION pattern, which accounts for sentences like *She poured water from the pitcher into the bowl*. This is represented in VerbNet as follows:

Syntactic representation:
NP V NP PP PP
Agent V Theme Source Location

Semantic representation:
MOTION (DURING(E), THEME)
NOT (**PREP** (START(E), THEME, LOCATION))
PREP (START(E), THEME, SOURCE)
PREP (END(E), THEME, LOCATION)
CAUSE (AGENT, E)

This representation details connections between the syntax and semantics using the semantic roles as links, indicating that the Agent is the Subject NP and has CAUSED the Event, and that the Theme is the Object NP and has a new LOCATION at the end of the event. These types of inferences provide the foundation for deep semantic analysis of text.

However, the specifications in VerbNet (as in other predicate lexicons, such as FrameNet, Baker et al., 1998; Fillmore et al., 2002) are seen as definitional – they are restricted to the core usages of the verbs that are valid for all verbs in the class. However, as noted above, people often use verbs productively, in ways that go beyond the boundaries of the verb class structure. It is important to correctly identify these productive usages when they occur, since they may be explicitly adding crucial inferences. If a construction is not recognized in the form of a syntactic frame in VerbNet, such inferences are not possible, greatly reducing VerbNet's utility and coverage. For example, creative uses of a verb, such as *She blinked the snow off her lashes*, would have no corresponding frame in *blink*'s class, the Hiccup class. It contains one intransitive frame:

NP V
Agent V
BODY_PROCESS (E, AGENT)
INVOLUNTARY (E, AGENT)

Sentences that coerce the meaning of *blink* to fit with a CM event would currently be misanalysed. One option might be to augment the Hiccup class with the CM frame from the Pour class, which would ensure that such sentences would be analyzed more accurately. However, given the productive nature of constructional coercion and its widespread applicability, the approach of adding any possible pattern to each class is not appropriate: this would undermine the definitional distinctions between classes and greatly lessen their usefulness.

Complicating the issue is the phenomenon of regular sense extensions (Dang et al., 1998), where what once may have been coercion has become entrenched and is now seen as a different sense of the verb. For example, the verbs in the Push class express the general meaning of exerting force on an object, such as *She pushed on the wall.* Often, the exertion of force moves the object, which can be expressed in a CM construction such as *She pushed the box across the room.* VerbNet accounts for this regular sense extension by including most of the Push verbs in the Carry class as well, which has the CM construction as one of its frames. Deciding when to include a verb in another class based on regular sense extensions, when to add a frame for a construction to a class, or when to reject the frame as a defining part of a class, is made difficult by the graded nature of matches between verbs and a construction. Our goal is to maintain the advantages of the class structure of VerbNet while enhancing it with a graded view of the applicability of a construction for each class. Noting the applicability of a construction will enable the inclusion of its appropriate semantic predicates, and the inferencing over them, which are currently not supported.

3 Our Proposal: Constructional Profiles

We aim to augment VerbNet with knowledge of constructions that are likely to be used extensibly with a range of verbs. Such extensible constructions will be core usages for some classes (such as the CM for the Pour class, as noted above) but will be less characteristic of the fundamental semantics of other verb classes (such as CM for the Hiccup class). We propose to identify such a construction and its varying roles in the different classes by using relevant statistics over usages of verbs in a corpus – what we call a *constructional profile*.

A constructional profile is a probabilistic assessment of the usage of a particular construction by the verbs in a class. We developed the following three measures to capture the relevant behavior, with the goal of providing both type- and token-based views of the behavior of a verb class with respect to a target construction:

P1	**P_{type}(X|C):** *probability that a verb type in class C is attested in construction X*
	P1 gives a type-based assessment, indicating how widespread the use of the construction is across the verb types in the class. For example, if 8 out of 10 members of a class appear with the construction, we might estimate P1 as 0.8.
P2	**P_{token}(X|C):** *probability that the instances of a typical verb in class C occur in construction X*
	P2 gives a token-based assessment, indicating, for a typical verb in the class, the relative amount of usage of the construction among all usages of the verb. For example, to estimate this, we might average across all verbs in the class, the percentage of tokens in this construction.
P3:	**P_{token}(X|X-verbs-in-C):** *same as P2 but considering only verbs that have been attested in construction X*
	P3 is the same as P2, but looking only at those verbs in the class that have an attested usage of the construction, removing verbs without attested usages.

We hypothesize that these measures will have high values for those classes for which the construction should be definitional; very low values for those classes that are not compatible with the construction; and varying values for those classes that allow coerced usages to a greater or lesser extent.

Although these probabilities are intuitively very simple, estimating them from corpus data poses a significant challenge. Since a construction is a pairing of form with meaning, recognizing the use of a particular construction is not simply a matter of determining the syntactic pattern of the usage; rather, certain semantic properties and relations must co-occur with the syntactic pattern. Earlier work has shown that a supervised learning method was able to discriminate potential usages of the CM construction given training sentences manually labeled as either CM or not (Hwang et al., 2010). Here, we aim instead to identify usages of the CM construction, but without requiring an expensive manual annotation effort. That is, we seek an unsupervised method for estimating the probabilities in P1–P3 above.

We approach this goal in steps as follows. First, we examine all the classes in VerbNet to see which allow the CM construction (Section 4). This anno-tation reveals shortcomings in VerbNet's representa-tion (classes that allow the CM construction but do not list it) and also provides a gold standard with which to evaluate our method of identifying an exten-sible construction using our constructional profiles. Second, we use the manually annotated CM construction data from Hwang et al. (2010) to estimate probabilities P1–P3 using maximum likelihood formulations (Section 5). An analysis of the predictive power of these constructional profile measures shows a good match with the distinctions made in the human annotation of the classes. Thus, our annotation based constructional profile measures show promise for identifying relevant behaviors of the construction across the classes. Third, we explore automatic methods for estimating the constructional profile measures without the need for manual annotations (Section 6). We use a hierarchical Bayesian model that learns verb classes from corpus data to provide unsupervised estimates of the constructional profiles, which also exhibit the relevant distinctions across the classes.

4 Annotating the VerbNet Resource

We begin with a manual examination of the resource and a thorough annotation of the status of each class with respect to the CM construction. This effort reveals a number of shortcomings in VerbNet, and the need for developing methods that can support the extension of VerbNet to better reflect the coercive uses of constructions across the classes. The annotation described here also forms the basis for the evaluation in the following sections of our new probabilistic measures, by motivating hypotheses about the expected patterns of use of the CM construction across the classes.

4.1 Annotation Guidelines and Results

The first goal of our manual annotation of VerbNet classes was to determine which classes currently represent CM in one of their frames. To this end, we identified which classes contain the following frame:

NP [Agent/Cause]-V-NP [Patient/Theme]-
PP [Source/Destination/Recipient/Location]

These frames correspond to classes such as Slide, with its frame NP-V-NP-PP.Destination: *Carla slid the books to the floor*. We also examined classes with the patterns NP-V-NP-PP.Oblique, NP-V-NP-PP. Theme2, and NP-V-NP-PP.Patient2. In these classes, annotators had to judge whether the final PP was compatible with CM. For example, the Breathe class contains the frame NP-V-NP.Theme-PP.Oblique, *The dragon breathed fire on Mary*, which is compatible with CM; whereas the same basic frame in the Other_cos class is not: NP V NP PP.Oblique, *The summer sun tanned her skin to a golden bronze.*

In addition, we annotated which classes were potentially compatible with CM for either all verbs in the class or only some verbs. The "some" classification has the drawback that it may be applied to classes with very different proportions of compatible verbs; while suitable for our exploratory work here, we plan to make finer distinctions in the future. A secondary determination was whether or not the class was compatible with CM as part of its core semantics, or if it was compatible with CM because it was coercible into the construction. A verb was considered "compatible with CM" and "not coerced" if the verb could be used in the CM construction and its semantics, as reflected in VerbNet's semantic predicates, involved a CAUSE predicate in combination with another predicate such as CONTACT, TRANSFER, (EN)FORCE, EMIT, TAKE_IN (predicates potentially involving movement along some path). For example, although CM is not already included as a frame for the Bend class containing the verb *fold*, the semantics of this class include CAUSE and CONTACT, and the verb can be used in a CM construction: *She folded the note into her journal*. Therefore, this class would have been considered "compatible with CM" but "not coerced". Conversely, a verb was considered "compatible with CM" and "coerced" if the verb could be used in the CM construction, yet its semantics, again as reflected in VerbNet, did not involve CAUSE and MOVEMENT ALONG A PATH (e.g., the verb *wiggle* of the Body_internal_motion class: *She wiggled her foot out of the boot*).

In summary, as presented in the table below, we annotated each class according to whether (1) the CM construction was already represented in VerbNet for this class, (2) the construction was possible for all, some, or none of the verbs in that class, and (3) the verbs of any class compatible with CM were coerced into the construction or not. The classification for (3) was made regardless of whether "all" verbs or only "some" were compatible with CM. This determination was made uniformly for a class: there were no classes in which only certain CM-compatible verbs were considered "coerced".

VN class example [# of classes like this]	CM in VN	CM is possible	CM is coerced
Banish [50]	Yes	All	No
Nonverbal_Expression [2]	Yes	All	Yes
Cheat [6]	Yes	Some	No
Exhale [18]	No	All	No
Hiccup [30]	No	All	Yes
Fill [46]	No	Some	No
Wish [54]	No	Some	Yes
Matter [64]	No	None	N/A

Notably, we identified 206 classes where at least some of the verbs in that class are compatible with the CM construction; however, VerbNet currently only recognizes the CM construction in 58 classes. There were several classes of interest: First, although it may seem unusual that CM is represented in 6 classes where we found that only "some" verbs were compatible with CM (e.g., Cheat class), these were cases where only more restricted subclasses are compatible with CM, and this syntactic frame is listed for that subclass. This suggests subclasses may provide a more precise characterization of which verbs are compatible with a construction.

Secondly, we identified 18 classes in which all verbs were compatible with CM without coercion; thus, these classes could likely be improved by the addition of the CM syntactic frame. Additionally, we found 30 classes in which all verbs are coercible into the CM construction; however, the actual likelihood of a verb in those classes occurring in a CM construction remains to be investigated in the following sections. Like those classes where it was determined that only "some" verbs are compatible with CM, usefully incorporating the CM construction into classes that require coercion relies on accurately determining the probability that verbs in those classes will actually appear in the CM construction.

For those classes in which "all" verbs are compatible with CM, our intuition was that some aspect of the verb's semantics either inherently includes or allows the verb to be coerced into the CM construction. Conversely, for those classes in which no verbs are compatible with CM, presumably some aspect of the verb's semantics is logically incompatible with CM. Although pinpointing precisely what aspect of a verb's semantics makes it compatible with CM may not be possible, we can investigate whether or not our intuitions are supported by examining the actual frequencies of CM constructions for given verbs or a given class.

4.2 Hypotheses

Using these annotations, we were able to develop two simple hypotheses.

Hypothesis 1: We expect the constructional profile measures for the CM construction in a given corpus to be highest for those classes in which all verbs were found to be compatible with CM; lower for classes in which only some verbs were found to be compatible; and lowest for classes in which no verbs were found to be compatible.

Hypothesis 2: We expect the constructional profile measures for the CM construction in a given corpus to be highest for verbs that fall into classes where CM is not considered coerced (for either some or all of the verbs in the class); lower for verbs that fall into classes in which the CM construction only works through coercion (for either some or all of the verbs in the class); and lowest for verbs that fall into classes in which no verbs are compatible with CM.

To investigate Hypothesis 1, we grouped the annotated classes according to whether all, some, or no verbs in the class are compatible with CM:

	Class example	# of classes
Allowed by All	Bring, Carry	106
Allowed by Some	Appoint, Lodge	100
Allowed by None	Try, Own	64

To investigate Hypothesis 2, we did a second grouping of the classes according to whether CM is not coerced, CM is coerced, or CM is simply not compatible with the class. This second grouping did not distinguish whether CM was compatible with "all" or "some" of the verbs in a given class.

	Class example	# of classes
Not Coerced	Put, Throw	120
Coerced	Floss, Wink	86
Not Compatible	Differ	64

5 Evaluation using Constructional Profiles

5.1 Annotated data description

Our research uses the data annotated for Hwang et al. (2010), in which 1800 instances in the form NP-V-NP-PP were identified in the Wall Street Journal portion of the Penn Treebank II (Marcus et al., 1994). Each instance of the data was single annotated with one of the two labels: CM or non-CM. The annotation guidelines were based on the CM analysis of Goldberg (1995).

Our analysis began with the same data but adopted a slightly narrower definition of CM. We diverged from the Hwang et al. (2010) study in the following two ways: (1) sentences where the object NP is an item that is created by the event denoted by the verb were not considered CM (e.g., *Mr. Pilson scribbled a frighteningly large figure on a slip of paper*, where the figure is created through the scribbling event); and (2) sentences in which movement is prevented were not considered CM (e.g., *He kept her at arm's length*). In agreement with Hwang et al., our annotation included both metaphorical senses (e.g., *[It] cast a shadow over world oil markets*) and literal senses (e.g., *The company moved the employees to New York*) of CM. Our annotation using the narrower guidelines resulted in 85.8% agreement with the original annotation.[1] The distribution of labels in our data is 21.8% for CM and 78.2% for NON-CM.

5.2 Annotated data description

Using statistics over the manually annotated data, we calculate maximum likelihood estimates of the three constructional profile measures introduced in Section 3, as follows. First, let the probability that a verb v is used in the CM construction be estimated as:

$$P(CM|v,C) = \frac{\#(\text{CM usages of } v \in C)}{\#(\text{CM+non-CM usages of } v \in C)}$$

That is, $P(CM|v,C)$ is estimated as the relative frequency of the CM construction for v out of all annotated usages of v that are labeled as class C. Now let C_{CM} be all verbs v in C with at least one usage annotated as CM; i.e.:

$$C_{CM} = \{v \in C \mid P(CM|v,C) > 0\}$$

Then we calculate estimates of P1–P3 as:

P1: $P_{type}(CM|C) = |C_{CM}|/|C|$
This measure indicates how widespread the use of CM is across the verb types in the class.

P2: $P_{token}(CM|C) = [\sum_{v \in C} P(CM|v,C)]/|C|$
The average over all verbs v in C of $P(CM|v,C)$
This indicates the relative amount of usage of CM among all usages of the verbs in the class.

P3: $P_{token}(CM|v,C) = [\sum_{v \in C_{CM}} P(CM|v,C))]/|C_{CM}|$
The average over all verbs v in C_{CM} of $P(CM|v,C)$
P3 narrows the P2 measure to only those verbs in the class for which there is an attested usage of CM.

[1]We found that 34.0% of the disagreements were directly due to the changes in annotation resulting from our two new criteria.

5.3 Analysis of the Constructional Profiles

The tables below provide a summary of the profile measures P1-P3 for the groups of VerbNet classes as defined in section 4.2. For each group listed, we report the averages of P1-P3 over all classes in the group where at least one verb in the class occurred in the data manually annotated for CM usage.

	P1	**P2**	**P3**
CM Allowed by All	0.413	0.323	0.437
CM Allowed by Some	0.087	0.078	0.224
CM Not Allowed	0.055	0.055	0.083

As seen here, the constructional profile measures over CM in the data corroborate our Hypothesis 1 (Section 4.2). All three measures on average are highest for the classes that fall into the "all allowed" group, next highest for those in the "some allowed" group, and lowest for the "not allowed" classes.

	P1	**P2**	**P3**
CM Non-Coerced	0.354	0.274	0.418
CM Coerced	0.091	0.091	0.185
CM Not Allowed[2]	0.056	0.056	0.083

Furthermore, the second table here confirms our expectations for Hypothesis 2 (Section 4.2). Again, all three measures on average are highest for classes that fall into the "non-coerced" group, next highest for classes in the "coerced" group (in which the construction is achievable only through coercion), and lowest for the "not allowed" group.

Thus, our two hypotheses are borne out, showing that our constructional profile measures, when estimated over manually annotated data, can be useful in capturing important distinctions among classes of verbs with regard to their usage in an extensible construction such as CM.

6 Automatic Creation of Constructional Profiles Using a Bayesian Model

Manually annotating a corpus for usages of a construction can be prohibitively expensive, so we also investigate the use of automatic methods to estimate constructional profile measures. By using a hierarchi-cal Bayesian model (HBM) that acquires latent prob-abilistic verb classes from corpus data, we provide unsupervised

[2] Note the non-zero values result from actual CM verb usages in the data belonging to classes believed to be not compatible with CM by VerbNet expert annotators.

estimates of the constructional profiles.

6.1 Overview of Model and Data

We use the HBM of Parisien & Stevenson (2011), a model that automatically acquires probabilistic knowledge about verb argument structure and verb classes from large-scale corpora. The model is based on a large body of research in nonparametric Bayesian topic modeling (e.g., Teh et al., 2004), a robust method of discovering syntactic and semantic structure in very large datasets. For each verb encountered in a corpus, the model provides an estimate of the verb's expected overall pattern of usage. By using latent probabilistic verb classes to influence these expected usage patterns, the model can, for example, estimate the probability that a verb like *blink* might occur in a CM construction, even if no such attested usages appear in the corpus.

In this preliminary study, we use the corpus data from Parisien & Stevenson (2011), since the model has been trained and evaluated on this data. As that study was aimed at modeling facts of child language acquisition, it uses child-directed speech from the Thomas corpus (Lieven et al., 2009), part of the CHILDES database (MacWhinney, 2000). In this preliminary study, we use their development dataset containing approx. 170,000 verb usages, covering approx. 1,400 verb types. (We reserve the test set for future experiments.) For each verb usage in the input, a number of features are automatically extracted that indicate the number and type of syntactic arguments occurring with the verb and general semantic properties of the verb. The semantic features are drawn from the set of VerbNet semantic predicates, such as CAUSE, MOTION, and CONTACT. These are automatically extracted from all classes compatible with the verb (with no sense disambiguation).

6.2 Measures for Constructional Profiles

Using the argument structure constructions, verb usage patterns and classes learned by the model, we estimate the three constructional profile measures in Section 3, as follows. First, we note that since the constructions acquired by the model are probabilistic in nature, a particular CM instance may be a partial match to more than one of the model's constructions.

For each verb in the input, we consider the likelihood of use of the CM construction to be the likelihood of a contrived frame intended to capture the important properties of a CM usage. F_{CM} is a usage taking a direct object and a prepositional phrase, and including the semantic features CAUSE and MOTION, with all other semantic features left unspecified. For a given verb v, we estimate the likelihood of this CM usage, over all constructions in the model, as follows:

$$P(F_{CM}|v) = \sum_{k} P(F_{CM}|k)P(k|v)$$

Here, $P(F_{CM}|k)$ is the likelihood of the CM usage F_{CM} being an instance of the probabilistic construction k, and $P(k|v)$ is the likelihood that verb v occurs with construction k. These component probabilities are estimated using the probability distributions acquired by the model and averaged over 100 samples from the Markov Chain Monte Carlo simulation, as described in Parisien & Stevenson (2011).

Now, we let C_{CM} be the set of verbs in VerbNet class C where the expected likelihood of a CM usage is non-negligible (akin to the set of verbs with attested usage in Section 5.2):

$$C_{CM} = \{v \in C \mid P(F_{CM}|v) > \lambda\}$$

where λ is a small threshold, here 0.0001. Note that since v is not disambiguated for class in our data, all usages of v contribute to this estimate.

The estimates of P1-P3 are comparable to those in Section 5.2. The difference is that since we are un-able to disambiguate individual usages of the verbs, each usage of v is considered to belong to all possible classes C of which v is a member. P1 is estimated as before; P2 and P3 are averages of $P(F_{CM}|v)$.

6.3 Analysis of the Constructional Profiles

The tables below provide a summary of the profile estimates P1-P3 for the groups of VerbNet classes as given in Section 4.2. For each group listed, we report the averages of P1-P3 over all classes in the group where at least one of the verbs in the class occurred in the training input to the model.

	P1	**P2**	**P3**
All allowed	0.569	0.0180	0.0250
Some allowed	0.449	0.0106	0.0192
Not allowed	0.363	0.0044	0.0079

These profile measures align with the hypotheses in Section 4.2 and with the measures based on manually annotated data in Section 5.2. The estimates are high-est for classes where all verbs permit the CM con-struction, second highest for classes where only some permit it, and lowest for classes that do not permit it.

	P1	**P2**	**P3**
CM non-coerced	0.546	0.0178	0.0260
CM coerced	0.458	0.0095	0.0167
CM not allowed	0.363	0.0044	0.0079

Again, the overall patterns of the profile measures align with Sections 4.2 and 5.2. The profile estimates are highest for classes annotated to be non-coerced usages of CM, second highest for coerced classes, and lowest for “not allowed”.

The measures show the overall differences among classes in the different groups (for both groupings) – i.e., the average behavior among classes in the different groups varies as we predicted. This indicates that the measures are tapping into aspects of construction usage that are relevant to making the desired distinctions in VerbNet, and validates the use of automatic techniques. However, there is a substantial amount of variability in these measures across the classes, so we also consider how well the estimates can predict the appropriate group for individual classes. That is, can we automatically predict whether the CM construction can be used by all, some, or none of the verbs in a given verb class, and can we predict whether such usages are coerced?

We consider the P3 measure as it provides the best separation among the class groupings. The tables below report precision (P), recall (R) and F-measures (F) for each group, where ‘all’ and ‘some’ have been collapsed. For exploratory purposes, we pick P3 = 0.006 as the value that optimizes F-measures of this classification. Future work will explore more principled means for setting these thresholds.

	P	R	F
CM allowed	0.880	0.742	0.806
CM not allowed	0.407	0.636	0.497

Only a 2-way distinction can be made reliably for the allowed grouping. The F-score of over 80% for the “allowed” label is very promising. The low precision for the “not allowed” case suggests that the model can’t generalize sufficiently due to sparse data.

	P	R	F
CM non-coerced	0.691	0.491	0.574
CM coerced	0.461	0.417	0.438
CM not allowed	0.406	0.709	0.517

We use thresholds of P3 = 0.021 to separate non-coerced from coerced classes, and P3 = 0.007 to separate coerced from not allowed classes. The model estimates show moderate success in distinguishing classes with coerced vs. non-coerced usage of the CM construction. However, our measures simply cannot distinguish non-occurrence due to semantic incompatibility from non-occurrence due to chance, given the expected low frequency of a novel coerced use of a construction. To separate the allowed cases into whether they are coerced or not requires a more detailed assessment of the semantic compatibility of the class, which means looking at finer-grained features of verb usages that are indicative of the semantic predicates compatible with the particular construction. Moreover, this kind of assessment likely needs to be applied on a verb-specific (and not just class-specific) level, in order to identify those verbs out of a potentially coercible class that are indeed coercible (i.e., identifying the coercible verbs in a class labeled as "some allowed").

7 Conclusion

Our investigation demonstrates that VerbNet does not currently represent the CM construction for all verbs or verb classes that are compatible with this construction, and the existing static representation of verbs is inadequate for analyzing extensions of verb meaning brought about by coercion. The utility of VerbNet would be greatly enhanced by an improved representation of constructions: specifically, the incorporation of probabilities that verbs in a given (sub)class would occur in a particular construction, and whether this constitutes a regular sense extension. This addition to VerbNet would increase the resource’s coverage of syntactic frames that are compatible with a given verb, and therefore enable appropriate inferences when coercion occurs. We have made preliminary steps towards developing this probabilistic distribution over both verb instances and classes, based on a large corpus. Unsupervised methods for estimating the probabilities achieve an F-score of over 80% in distinguishing the classes that allow the target construction. However, making distinctions among coerced and non-coerced cases will require us to go beyond these class-based probabilities to finer-grained, corpus-based assessments of a verb’s semantic compatibility with a coercible construction.

To move beyond these preliminary findings, we must therefore shift our focus to the behavior of individual verbs. Additionally, to reduce the impact of errors resulting from low-frequency verbs and classes, we plan to expand our research to more data, specifically the OntoNotes TreeBank data (Weischedel et al., 2011). Finally, to achieve our ultimate goal of creating a lexicon that can flexibly account for a variety of constructions, we will examine other constructions as well. While determining the set of coercible constructions in a language is itself a topic of current research, we propose initially to include the widely recognized CAUSE-RECEIVE and WAY constructions in addition to CM.

References

Baker, Collin F., Charles J. Fillmore, and John B. Lowe. 1998. The Berkeley FrameNet Project. *Proceedings of the 17th International Conference on Computational Linguistics (COLING/ACL-98),* pp. 86–90, Montreal.

Dang, HoaTrang, Karin Kipper, Martha Palmer, and Joseph Rosenzweig. 1998. Investigating regular sense extensions based on intersective Levin classes. *Proceedings of COLING-ACL98*, pp. 293–299.

Fillmore, Charles J., Christopher R. Johnson, and Miriam R.L. Petruck. 2002. Background to FrameNet. *International Journal of Lexicography,* 16(3):235-250.

Gerber, Matthew, and Joyce Y. Chai. 2010. Beyond NomBank: A study of implicit arguments for nominal predicates. *Proceedings of the 48th Annual Meeting of the Association of Computational Linguistics,* pp. 1583–1592, Uppsala, Sweden, July.

Goldberg, A. E. 1995. *Constructions: A construction grammar approach to argument structure*. Chicago: University of Chicago Press.

Goldberg, A. E. 2006. *Constructions at work: The nature of generalization in language*. Oxford: Oxford University Press.

Goldberg, A. E. To appear. Corpus evidence of the viability of statistical preemption. *Cognitive Linguistics*.

Hwang Jena D., Rodney D. Nielsen and Martha Palmer. 2010. Towards a domain-independent semantics: Enhancing semantic representation with construction grammar. *Proceedings of Extracting and Using Constructions in Computational Linguistic Workshop*, held with NAACL HLT 2010, Los Angeles, June.

Kay, P., and C. J. Fillmore. 1999. Grammatical constructions and linguistic generalizations: The What's X Doing Y? construction. *Language,* 75:1–33.

Kipper, Karin, Anna Korhonen, Neville Ryant, and Martha Palmer. 2008. A large-scale classification of English verbs. *Language Resources and Evaluation Journal,* 42:21–40.

Langacker, R. W. 1987. *Foundations of cognitive grammar: Theoretical prerequisites*. Stanford, CA: Stanford University Press.

Lapata, M., and A. Lascarides. 2003. Detecting novel compounds: The role of distributional evidence. *Proceedings of the 11th Conference of the European Chapter of the Association for Computational Linguistics*(EACL03), pp.235–242. Budapest, Hungary.

Levin, B. 1993.*English Verb Classes and Alternations: A Preliminary Investigation*. Chicago: Chicago University Press.

Lieven, E., D. Salomo, and M. Tomasello. 2009. Two-year-old children's production of multiword utterances: A usage-based analysis. *Cognitive Linguistics* 20(3):481–507.

MacWhinney, B. 2000.*The CHILDES Project: Tools for analyzing talk* (3rd ed., Vol. 2: The Database). Erlbaum.

Màrquez, L., X. Carreras, K. Litkowski, and S. Stevenson. 2008. Semantic role labeling: An introduction to the special issue. *Computational Linguistics,* 34(2): 145–159.

Martha Palmer, Jena D. Hwang, Susan Windisch Brown, Karin Kipper Schuler and Arrick Lanfranchi. 2009. Leveraging lexical resources for the detection of event relations. *Proceedings of the AAAI 2009 Spring Symposium on Learning by Reading*, Stanford, CA, March.

Palmer, Martha, Daniel Gildea, and Paul Kingsbury.2005. The Proposition Bank: An annotated corpus of semantic roles. *Computational Linguistics,* 31(1):71–106.

Parisien, Christopher, and Suzanne Stevenson. 2011. To appear in *Proceedings of the 33rd Annual Meeting of the Cognitive Science Society,* Boston, MA, July.

Pustejovsky, J., and E. Jezek. 2008. Semantic coercion in language: Beyond distributional analysis. *Italian Journal of Linguistics/RivistaItaliana di Linguistica* 20(1): 181–214.

Shi, Lei, and Rada Mihalcea. 2005. Putting pieces together: Combining FrameNet, VerbNet and WordNet for robust semantic parsing. *Proceedings of the 6th International Conference on Intelligent Text Processing and Computational Linguistics,* Mexico City, Mexico.

Swier, R., and S. Stevenson. 2004. Unsupervised semantic role labeling. *Proceedings of the 2004 Conf. on Empirical Methods in Natural Language Processing,* pp. 95–102, Barcelona, Spain.

Teh, Y. W., M. I. Jordan, M. J.Beal, and D. M.Blei.2006. Hierarchical Dirichlet processes. *Jrnl of the American Statistical Asscn*, 101(476): 1566–1581.

Weischedel, R., E. Hovy, M. Marcus, M. Palmer, .R. Belvin, S. Pradan, L. Ramshaw and N. Xue. 2011.OntoNotes: A Large Training Corpus for Enhanced Processing. In Part 1: Data Acquisition and Linguistic Resources of *The Handbook of Natural Language Processing and Machine Translation: Global Automatic Language Exploitation,* Eds.: Joseph Olive, Caitlin Christianson, John McCary. Springer Verlag, pp. 54-63.

Zaenen, A., C. Condoravdi, and D. G. Bobrow. 2008. The encoding of lexical implications in VerbNet. *Proceedings of LREC 2008,* Morocco, May.

Author Index